Perspectives on Theological Education

Essays in Honor of C. Penrose St. Amant

edited by
Walter B. Shurden

Gateway Seminary Library

MERCER UNIVERSITY PRESS

ISBN 0-86554-370-4

Perspectives on Theological Education
Essays in Honor of C. Penrose St. Amant
Copyright © 1989
Mercer University Press
Macon GA 31207
All rights reserved
Printed in the United States of America

The paper used in this publication meets
the minimum requirements of American National Standard
for Information Sciences—Permanence of Paper
for Printed Library Materials, ANSI Z39.48-1984.

CONTENTS

Editorial Introduction 5

C. Penrose St. Amant:
A Chronology 7
Lynn E. May, Jr.,
Southern Baptist Historical Commission, Nashville TN 37203-3620

C. Penrose St. Amant:
An Interpretation of the Man 11
Frank Stagg,
The Southern Baptist Theological Seminary (Emeritus), Louisville KY 40280

C. Penrose St. Amant:
Teacher and Historian 27
Claude Howe,
New Orleans Baptist Theological Seminary, New Orleans LA 70126

C. Penrose St. Amant:
Dean at Southern, 1959–1969 41
E. Glenn Hinson,
The Southern Baptist Theological Seminary, Louisville KY 40280

C. Penrose St. Amant:
President at Rüschlikon 53
G. Keith Parker,
Baptist Theological Seminary, 8803 Rüschlikon, Switzerland

C. Penrose St. Amant:
Preacher of the Gospel 65
W. Morgan Patterson,
Georgetown College, Georgetown KY 40324

C. Penrose St. Amant:
Interpreter of the Baptist Vision 73
Walter B. Shurden,
Mercer University, Macon GA 31207

C. Penrose St. Amant:
A Bibliography 89
Lynn E. May, Jr.,
Southern Baptist Historical Commission, Nashville TN 37203-3620

EDITORIAL INTRODUCTION

No more beautiful and accurate introduction to Penrose St. Amant as teacher and person can be written than the poem written by the late Don B. Harbuck, one of St. Amant's former students. You will find the poem on pages twenty-four and twenty-five of this volume. If you studies under St. Amant or if you know anything at all about the man, you need no interpreter for the poem. Penrose is, as Harbuck wrote, "a strange sort of saint." He is both "suave and secular" and "a holy man incognito." As a church history teacher of would-be ministers, St. Amant was a compassionate prophet. "He shocked us gently with those shrines," remembered Harbuck. And he did it with "style," with what Frank Stagg describes in his masterful introductory article in this volume as "class."

> "Profiled pensively against the chalkboard
>   lost in vision
>   eyes fixed fleetingly
>   beyond the class
>   on some hidden horizon"

are Harbuck's words that elicit an irresistible image of any student who ever sat in St. Amant's classes.

While Harbuck's poem accurately described St. Amant as teacher, it did not provide a comprehensive portrait of the man. A masterful teacher, St. Amant has been and is so much more. Behind his teaching is a careful, broad scholarship. And what an inspiring preacher/speaker! And what a genius of an administrator as Dean at Southern Seminary and President at Rüschlikon. Ernest T. Campbell once preached a baccalaureate sermon at Princeton Seminary entitled, "They Also Serve Who Lead." Lauding the administrative side of ministry, Campbell's sermon title certainly captures a major part of Penrose St. Amant's contribution to theological education.

Few, if any, leaders in theological education in this generation of Baptists have been as versatile as Penrose St. Amant. After serving as a major shaping force at the New Orleans Baptist Theological Seminary in the 1940s and 1950s, he helped put Southern Seminary on its feet again in the 1960s. Following his tenure at Southern, he gave crucial leadership to European Baptist theological education at Rüschlikon, Switzerland. His life has been dedicated to Baptist theological education. Baptists are the better for it.

Walter B. Shurden

C. PENROSE ST. AMANT: A CHRONOLOGY

LYNN E. MAY, JR.
Southern Baptist Historical Commission, Nashville TN 37203-3620

1915	Born 8 April Gonzales, Louisiana
1921	Entered elementary school at Gonzales, Louisiana
1922	Converted and baptized into the Gonzales Baptist Church
1932	Graduated from Gonzales High School; entered Louisiana College, Pineville, Louisiana
1934	Elected President of Louisiana Baptist Student Union
1936	Graduated from Louisiana College (B.A.); entered Louisiana State University, Baton Rouge, Louisiana
1937	Graduated from Louisiana State University (M.A.); entered New Orleans Baptist Theological Seminary, New Orleans, Louisiana
1939	Studied at Union Theological Seminary and Columbia University during summers of 1939, 1943, 1944, 1946
1939–1940	Served on Executive Board of Louisiana Baptist Convention
1940	Received the master of theology (Th.M.) degree from New Orleans Baptist Theological Seminary
1942	Ordained 15 May as minister of the gospel by Gonzales Baptist Church, Gonzales, Louisiana; received doctor of theology (Th.D.) degree from New Orleans Baptist Theological Seminary; employed by Hannibal LaGrange College, Hannibal, Missouri, as professor of religion
1943–1959	Taught at New Orleans Baptist Theological Seminary, first as an instructor, then as associate professor, and from 1948–1959 as professor of church history
1945	Married Jessie Louise Davis of Brownsville, Tennessee, 21 November
1945–1947	Served as member of History Committee of Southern Baptist Convention
1947–1951	Member of Board of Directors of Southern Baptist Historical Society

1948	His first book, *A Short History of Louisiana Baptists*, published by Broadman Press
1949	Interim pastor of First Baptist Church, Forest, Mississippi; St. Charles Avenue Baptist Church, New Orleans, Louisiana, 1949–1950
1951–1955	Louisiana member of Historical Commmission of the Southern Baptist Convention
1952	Received doctor of philosophy (Ph.D.) degree from Edinburgh University, Edinburgh, Scotland; interim pastor of First Baptist Church, Woodville, Texas (also in 1958)
1954	Delivered Holland Lectures at Southwestern Baptist Theological Seminary; lectures published by the seminary as *Christian Faith and History*
1954–1958	Area editor and writer for *Encyclopedia of Southern Baptists*, volumes 1 and 2
1955	Awarded honorary doctor of laws (LL.D.) degree by Louisiana College; delivered Layne Lectures at New Orleans Baptist Theological Seminary; named director, Bank of Gonzales, Gonzales, Louisiana
1955–1959	Member, Executive Board, Greater New Orleans Federation of Churches
1956	Preacher for weekly radio program, "Faith for Life," New Orleans, Louisiana; *A History of Louisiana Baptist Student Union* published by Broadman
1957	Distinguished Service Award, Louisiana Baptist Student Union
1957–1959	Board of Trustees, Union Theological Seminary, New Orleans, Louisiana
1959–1969	Dean, School of Theology, Southern Baptist Theological Seminary
1959–1972	David T. Porter Professor of Church History, Southern Baptist Theological Seminary
1961	*A History of the Presbyterian Church in Louisiana* published; awarded honorary doctor of divinity (D.D.) degree by Mercer University, Macon, Georgia
1963–1967	Chairman, Historical Commission of the Southern Baptist Convention
1964	Additional study at Paris (Sorbonne), Protestant Theological Faculty of Paris
1969–1970	Area editor and writer for *Encyclopedia of Southern Baptists*, vol. 3

A CHRONOLOGY

1970	Distinguished Alumnus Award, New Orleans Baptist Theological Seminary
1970–1971	Visiting Professor of Church History, Baptist Theological Seminary, Rüschlikon, Switzerland
1971–1977	Professor of Church History and President of Baptist Theological Seminary, Rüschlikon, Switzerland
1972	Delivered Carver-Barnes Lectures at Southeastern Baptist Theological Seminary
1974–1977	Treasurer of Switzerland Mission, Foreign Mission Board of the Southern Baptist Convention; member of Baptist/Reformed Theological Consultation
1977	Delivered C. H. Jones Memorial Lectures, Union University, Jackson, Tennessee
1979	Taught as guest professor at Southern Baptist Theological Seminary (also 1980, 1981–82); taught as guest professor at Golden Gate Baptist Theological Seminary (also 1980, 1981, 1982, 1983–84)
1980	Taught at Rumanian Baptist Pastors' Conference, Constanta, Rumania; preached in Baptist churches in Rumania and Hungary; taught in Summer Institute of Theological Education, Rüschlikon, Switzerland
1982–1988	Senior Professor of Church History, Southern Baptist Theological Seminary
1983	Taught in Summer Institute of Theological Education, Rüschlikon, Switzerland
1984	Delivered H. I. Hester Lectures to Association of Southern Baptist Colleges and Schools
1985–1986	Guest Professor of Church History, Southwestern Baptist Theological Seminary
1986	Deere Lectures presented at Golden Gate Baptist Theological Seminary
1987	Colvin Distinguished Professor of Religion, Louisiana College in spring semester; delivered Walter Pope Binns Lectures at William Jewell College; suffered heart attack November 17; underwent triple bypass surgery December 15

C. PENROSE ST. AMANT:
AN INTERPRETATION OF THE MAN

FRANK STAGG
The Southern Baptist Theological Seminary (Emeritus), Louisville KY 40280

Some years ago I walked into Office Services at The Southern Baptist Theological Seminary and at once realized that those there were talking about Dean Penrose St. Amant, not surprisingly in a most positive way. Someone summed it up by saying, "They call it class!" Whether or not this is the best word for it, the intention behind the term is valid as one tries to say something not easily said in any word or many words. To those who have known Penrose close up, in formal and casual situations, he does have what those in Office Services intended to say by the word "class."

"Class" may include style, but it is more than that. Style can be developed, and it may or may not reflect the real quality of the person bearing it. As used here, "class" stands for something deeper, a quality of being and not just a manner of existence. "Class," as used here, is not to be confused with the social idea of "first class" as opposed to "second class" or less. What is esteemed in Penrose St. Amant as "class" is not something competitive, gained at another's expense. It is an inherent quality, not something sought. It is something sensed by others whether they know how to define it or not.

"Class" implies excellence, but it is more. Many excel in some way or in many ways, yet do not have that quality known as class. It is an elusive something that sets a person apart and elicits attention, respect, admiration, and more. It may include "charisma" (itself a gift as the Greek *charis* implies), but it is more. It is more than charm. In Penrose it includes excellence in the various aspects of personhood.

Penrose is "one of a kind." Of people generally it is not uncommon to hear that someone is like someone else. Penrose is not like anyone else. He has qualities in common with others, but he is *sui generis,* unique. We sometimes say that a person reminds us of some other person, but Penrose does not remind us of anyone else. When we see or think of him. we are reminded only of Penrose. Such is his uniqueness. Even the name Penrose sets him apart. Although the name is known outside his family and prominently within his family, to thousands who know him, it is sufficient simply to say "Penrose" and all understand the referent. Within the family and to some close friends, he is known affectionately as "Penny." To his wife Jessie and to most of his friends, he is "Penrose."

Difference in Penrose does not imply indifference to others. In fact, family and friendships are cherished by him as primary and indispensable. The polar claims are there in creative tension: individual identity which requires its own space and privacy, and the bonds of family and friendship.

Penrose has a wide circle of friends internationally and a closer circle as near as kin. Some go back to his early years, including students who know him simply as "Prof." Any listing would fail in its incompletion, omitting some as close as those listed. Close friendships include peers in higher education and others who went no further than grade or high school. Taking the above-mentioned risk simply to illustrate, there was the late Rufus C. Harris, close friend since the latter's presidency of Tulane University; and there is Winfred Hurst, carpenter and neighbor, this friendship having begun in a chance meeting in a lumber yard more than a quarter-century ago. There is Günter Wagner, Dr. theol. from the University of Zürich and international scholar; and there is Welby Collins, security guard at Southern Seminary, both among cherished houseguests at "Tree Tops" in coastal Mississippi. Friendships for Penrose are not competitive; each has its own special meaning.

FAMILY HERITAGE

There is no adequate understanding of Penrose St. Amant apart from his family heritage. Those of us who knew his father and mother in Gonzales, Louisiana, recognize the rootage to much in the quality found in Penrose. I found this through many hours in the home in Gonzales, especially Sunday afternoons between morning and evening services in the home church, where I often served as interim pastor.

The deep piety and quiet, gentle spirit of Penrose's mother, known in Gonzales as "Miss Lydia," left their marks upon her son. Lydia Landry descended from the Acadian French who settled in south Louisiana in the eighteenth century, driven out of Canada when the English took over from the French. Lydia St. Amant was a devout Roman Catholic, and as a young woman she was organist in her church. Penrose still has his mother's prayer book in French. When Lydia Landry and Lyle Penrose St. Amant were married in the Catholic Church in Prairieville, Louisiana, he was Presbyterian. He gave her a Bible at a time when Catholics in Louisiana did not have Bibles, not even priests. Through reading the Bible and other influences, Lydia became a Baptist. She was baptized in the Amite River in 1915. Six years later Penrose's father was converted to the Baptist faith. Within a year, Penrose himself made his profession of faith and was baptized. With this background, none need apprise Penrose of the primacy of the Bible for Christian faith or Baptist persuasion. For the St. Amants, the Bible is not a book to debate; it changed the direction of their religious pilgrimage.

Through his parents, Penrose has a long heritage in both Roman Catholic and Protestant traditions. As just seen, his mother was a devout Catholic before her conversion to the Baptist faith. The thoroughly French St. Amant line from which Penrose came would lead one to assume that these, too, were

Roman Catholic. His great-great-great-great grandfather was Jean Francois Daspit de St. Amand, married to Marie Francoise DuBuisson, coming to Louisiana about 1720. From these came Pierre Daspit de St. Amant, married to Marie Anne Carmouche; next were Alexis Alexandre St. Amant, married to Marguerite Zeringue, he a major in the Battle of New Orleans; next came Venance St. Amant, married to Amelie Asselin, he the first physician to practice in his part of Louisiana; next came Pierre Telesphore St. Amant, married to Elizabeth Montgomery, grandparents to Penrose. But the religious identity is not necessarily as might appear.

The St. Amant line from which Penrose comes, including Bernard Daspit (Despy, Despie) and his wife, "the noble lady" Anne de Saint-Amand, is traceable back to Languedoc, France; and this may give the clue to the non-Catholic tradition on the side of Penrose's father. Languedoc was a cradle of liberty, free thought, and intellectual progress long before the Reformation, a stronghold for the Albigenses and others asserting their independence of the Catholic Church by the twelfth and thirteenth centuries. It was in this part of France that Calvinism found ready reception. Although the religious identity of the early Daspits and Saint-Amands cannot be documented here, the likelihood is that the Protestantism which appears no later than Penrose's grandfather and father derived from this background. This heritage may well be a proper clue to understanding Penrose St. Amant.

Significantly, Penrose is the only Baptist to preach in the historic Saint Louis Cathedral in New Orleans since W. B. Johnson, first President of the Southern Baptist Convention. On 8 May 1980, Penrose preached there on the subject, "The Church: A Community of Celebration," preaching from Psalm 150 and Luke 4:32. He was invited because of his competence for the occasion and the recognition that he can transcend confessional differences without compromise to his own Baptist identity. Traditions reaching back to Languedoc, France may have helped prepare Penrose for this role.

Penrose's father was the youngest of thirteen children, their father a physician, Dr. Pierre Telesphore St. Amant. Penrose does not remember his paternal grandfather as a religious man but rather as concentrating upon his medical practice. Of his thirteen children, one became a physician, one a dentist, and one a lawyer, all university graduates. Thus for Penrose, higher education was as normal as three meals a day. Alongside his mother's quiet piety was his father's more outgoing spirit. His independence, imagination, creativity, drive, courage, and deep devotion to God, to his family, to his church, to his community, and a special feeling for little children and disadvantaged people are qualities not lost on Penrose.

Born on 8 April 1915 Penrose thus reached college at the bottom of "the depression," entering Louisiana College at age seventeen in September 1932. Only those who experienced the depression of the 1930s really understand it. A dime could get a pair of trousers pressed, but many could not spare the dime.

Campus work at twenty-five cents an hour lacked no applicants. A student with an automobile was almost unknown, but Penrose had one. He also was authorized to write checks at his own discretion on his father's bank account. In fact, his father had a major share in ownership of the Bank of Gonzales, having been a co-founder. Penrose neither concealed nor advertised his advantage. That simply was a part of his heritage and identity, and he made neither much nor little of it.

Penrose's father, Dr. L. P. St. Amant, "Dr. Pen" to many, was a dentist in Gonzales; and his uncle Clyde was a lawyer and judge. These brothers and P. S. Berteau, with $20,000 among them, founded the Bank of Gonzales about 1920. They did this not for personal gain or power but because Gonzales needed a bank. "Dr. Pen" continued his dental practice until 1933, never rejecting a client for that one's lack of a fee. He succeeded Mr. Berteau as President of the bank in 1933 and so served until his death in 1970. In his latter years, Dr. Pen approached Penrose about becoming his successor as president of the Bank, but Penrose firmly declined, his vocational sense being in another direction. Penrose has participated routinely as a Director since 1955, even during his years in Rüschlikon, flying back for regular meetings of the Board of Directors.

The material advantages known to Penrose as a college student in the depression and in the years since owe much to his father's advantage that resulted from seeking to serve a community. Penrose's disposition and ability to keep advantage under control and put it to responsible service reflect both his family heritage and his own personal character.

Penrose's parents could have built a mansion in Gonzales, but they chose to live in a simple, two-bedroom house, frame with a tin roof and an open porch with its much-used swing, a house much like that of many French families in south Louisiana. Such a house met their needs, and they asked no more. Generous with others, their own sense of needs was very modest. They neither despised the material nor stood under its tyranny. They controlled it; it did not own them.

A typewritten letter dated "Oct. 24th 1918," now brown and fragile with age, reflects much about the home from which Penrose came. The letter is from "L.P. St. Amant, DDS" to "Mr. H. M. Picard, Pres. of Red Cross," written during the influenza epidemic of 1918. Dr. St. Amant reports to the Red Cross "cases of influenza seen and given attention by me" as he assisted physicians in Gonzales. In the 10-day period covered by the letter, Penrose's father attended to 170 persons with influenza, then highly contagious and often fatal. This is the dentist who became a banker. This is the man with whom I enjoyed many Sunday afternoon hours, talking religion and life.

Life for Penrose took new directions, and his lifestyle differed considerably. The house at 909 Ursulines Avenue in the French Quarter in New Orleans, the rustic homes on the Ohio River in Kentucky, and "Tree Tops" on a bluff on the fabulously beautiful Rotten Bayou (*sic!*) in coastal Mississippi were not patterned after the Gonzales home, yet bear some continuity with it. World travels, opera, symphony, stage plays in New York, and avid involvement in sports did not derive from Gonzales. The long journey from Gonzales to Rüschlikon via Louisiana College, Baptist Bible Institute, L.S.U., Union Theological Seminary and Columbia University, Hannibal LaGrange College, New Orleans Baptist Theological Seminary, the University of Edinburgh, the Sorbonne, The University of Zürich, and Southern Seminary owes much to the family heritage; but to a great extent it reflects the individual identity of Penrose, and of course Jessie.

PENROSE AND JESSIE

Brooks Hays, Congressman from Arkansas and distinguished Baptist layman as well as humorist, said, "Behind every successful man is a loyal wife and a surprised mother-in-law." This could be said of Penrose only with careful correction. First, there are no persons surprised at his successes, mother-in-law or otherwise. Next, there is Jessie! She has not been so much behind Penrose as alongside him. Theirs is a partnership marriage in the fullest sense. In marriage they brought already significant achievements to new dimensions of fulfillment.

Until he met Jessie, Penrose was a seeming candidate for bachelorhood; and already he loomed large on the scene in New Orleans as a scholar on the cutting edge for Baptists. Jessie, too, was already established in a responsible work, upon graduation from Blue Mountain College having come to Southern Baptist Hospital in New Orleans as secretary to the superintendent. They met, they married on 21 November 1945, and they have grown together. Probably they alone can sort it out as to precisely how their gifts have together yielded the results in their partnership in marriage and ministry.

In the strange mathematics of marriage, where "the two shall become one flesh," one plus one equals one. It is sometimes mistakenly said that outside marriage one is only a partial or unfilled person, as though in marriage one-half plus one-half equals one. In truth, two half-persons never make a marriage. Penrose and Jessie brought the fullness of each into union, with the happy results that followed. Neither became the other. They retain their individual identity and integrity, in some ways quite unlike. With this are the bonds which make them one. Penrose goes on with his scholarly pursuits and varied life interests. Jessie is homemaker in the best sense of that term, keeping the home in running order, and oh those gourmet meals! But she is far more than this to the partnership. Not always apparent to the public, she is deeply involved in all that Penrose does, both planning and implementation. When decisions are to be made, it is not uncommon to hear Penrose say, "Let me talk with Jessie." Not only does she protect his privacy and see that he has the comforts and facilities for his ministry, but she shares in their pilgrimage of faith and ministry, including special attention to *their* students. Penrose doubtless could have done well as a bachelor, but with Jessie he has done better.

A DOG'S BEST FRIEND

Ancient wisdom has it that a dog is man's best friend. Although exaggerated, this struggles to say something true. It is no accident that a dog is called "Fido," Latin for faithful, a canine quality. The reverse is also true, that a man may be a dog's best friend.

Penrose and Jessie have had four dogs since 1946, and that story is illuminating for an understanding of the St. Amants. These relationships are neither to be blown out of proportion nor to be written off as incidental. These four beautiful dogs were Copper, a golden cocker spaniel (1946–57); Pierre, a black toy French poodle (1957–74); Basel, a highly pedigreed Yorkshire terrier (1977–81); and presently Swiss Boy, from the same kennel as Basel in Switzerland (1981–).

To Penrose, his dog is more than a pet. He reserves ultimate reverence for God alone, but he has something approaching reverence for life itself, including "all creatures great and small." His theology and practice affirm the Genesis perspective, that when God looked upon his creation he called it good. His special attachment to Swiss Boy and his predecessors is not isolated: it is one focus reflecting a more inclusive attitude toward all life.

Penrose is a Christian theist, so by no means a pantheist or secularist. Neither is he a dualist like Marcion, with the latter's disdain for God's creation. Marcion saw creation as evil, Christ being for him the Redeemer to save us from creation and our own creaturehood. Such dualism is untenable to Penrose, theologically and existentially. With his faith in God as Creator/Redeemer is his biblically holistic view of reality, in which is grounded his reverence for all life. As for Francis of Assisi, so for Penrose, all creatures great and small are "all creatures of our God and King."

Something in Penrose's heritage turned him in boyhood toward his reverence for all life. Years ago I heard him relate with regret a story from his boyhood, his killing of a mockingbird with a .22 rifle. This was a normal act for a boy in his home town, but when he saw the dead bird he was in anguish at what he had done—killed a mockingbird! He has never killed a bird or animal since. This reverence for life includes forests as well. Visitors welcomed to the fifty acres of forest surrounding "Tree Tops" do not include bulldozers or chainsaws.

Penrose speaks of a "cosmic agony," the innocent suffering of creatures at every level. Such suffering in the world compels for him a theological struggle, a "theodicy" which is never completely resolved.

The affection and tender care given their dogs reflect much about Penrose and Jessie. Photographs of each dog adorn the walls at Tree Tops. Their dog almost invariably travels with them, in this land and abroad. Copper was a carefully selected gift from Jessie to Penrose. Copper died of cancer, suffering much in the last of his eleven years with the St. Amants. Penrose and Jessie suffered, too. Pierre lived for almost eighteen years, extremely old for a dog; and in his last years he received a special diet and vitamins, with daily and loving care. Basel's death—he was killed by a larger dog—was a trauma for Penrose and Jessie. A visiting professor then at Golden Gate Baptist Theological Seminary, Penrose cancelled his classes that day. By transatlantic telephone, he persuaded the kennel in Basel, Switzerland to sell him another Yorkshire Terrier, one that had been reserved for the kennel's own breeding. Is a dog man's best friend? That may be argued; but at least four dogs could attest that Penrose and Jessie were their best friends.

As indicated above, if isolated, this would be of little significance. It is not isolated, for it is both a focus to a larger value system and a reflection of a broader grounding. Their love for dogs is one window among many through which one may gain some perception of who Penrose and Jessie are.

SPORTS AND HUMOR

Sports play an important role in the life of Penrose. Examples of his fascination with sports appear in lectures and sermons, as in a chapel message, "How Tall is a Giant?"[1] He introduced this talk with a dramatic story from Little League Baseball, where a team of small boys from Mexico won a national title in the United States. A spectator now, Penrose was a participant in earlier years. His freshman football at Louisiana College was less than spectacular (his team lost to what now is the University of Southwest Louisiana by the score of 140–0), but he became accomplished in golf, shooting regularly in the seventies in his best years. The game was fun for him, especially in the company of friends.

Penrose is an avid follower of football, basketball, baseball, golf, and sports generally. He enjoys televised games, where a good seat brings one closer to a game of football than a ticket on the fifty-yard line.[2] He also enjoys the excitement of being in the stands for select games. He will secure tickets months in advance for the Sugar Bowl, Super Bowl, or the NCAA "Final Four." He will drive hundreds of miles for a choice game, especially if L.S.U. is playing. Unlike theological controversy, athletic contests for him are fun. It should be no surprise that he has an aversion to religious quarrels and a fascination with competitive sports.

---

[1]*Professor in the Pulpit*, ed. by W. Morgan Patterson and Raymond Bryan Brown (Nashville: Broadman Press, 1963) 1–7.

[2]See Penrose St. Amant, "Communicating the Gospel in the Eighties," *The Quarterly Review* 41:3 (April-May-June, 1981): 67.

Although positive towards sports, Penrose is troubled about "why Americans work so hard at play . . . and why there is no satisfactory theology of leisure in spite of the widespread interest today in games, television, and weekend cottages in the country."[3] His value system also enters into his feeling about sports, giving rise to serious tension. He is incensed by the enormous inequity between salaries in sports and salaries/wages for most people. He is not happy with paying a young athlete millions of dollars for being able to outrun an opponent or throw a round ball through a hoop, while many receive by comparison a mere pittance for their skills in more serious areas of life.

Penrose has a strong sense of humor, and he can laugh with people in the anomalies and absurdities of life. A case in point comes from our student days in college. It took place in Volunteer Band, comprised of young men and women dedicated to Christian service. Addressing us was a fellow student whose reach in vocabulary exceeded his grasp. Intending to compliment us, he said, "I am honored to speak to this motley group." This "motley" group included Penrose, G. Earl Guinn, my brother Paul L. Stagg, and others who became distinguished in various fields. Penrose can still laugh over this one.

Another instance occurred in a graduate oral examination in New Orleans. The student was being examined in the area of Gnosticism, and Penrose wanted him to mention the work bearing the Greek title *Pistis Sophia* (*Faith Wisdom*). Unable to come up with it, the student received encouragement and hints from Penrose. Suddenly, with a sense of triumph, thinking that he had dredged it up, the student shouted, "*Ipso facto!*" Penrose shook with laughter but dealt mercifully with the student as we laughed, not at the student, but at the incongruities in the human scene. Penrose, takes his students seriously, but he helps us us all not to take ououourselves too seriously.

A RENAISSANCE MAN?

Walter B. Shurden once said in conversation, "Penrose St. Amant is a Renaissance man, more a generalist than a specialist." What Walter intended by this accords with an impression I have had from our years together. However, for both of us the term would have to be carefully qualified if applied to Penrose. To the extent that "Renaissance man" may imply the liberation of the human mind and spirit from ecclesiastical or other tyranny; a recovery of the "classic" past; affirmation of the dignity, freedom, and responsibility of the human being; and attention to literature, music, and art, as well as science; Penrose may be said to be a "Renaissance man." Of course, he is first and always a Christian who sees "man" (generic usage) as both in the image

---

[3]"The Impact of Religion on the Shaping of American Values," *Review and Expositor* 73:1 (Winter 1976): 62.

of God and crippled by sin. He would reject the idea that man can reconstitute himself apart from God.

There are elements in the Renaissance, itself highly pluralistic, which would not characterize Penrose, certainly not any secular expression of its humanism. Penrose has from his early years done battle with secularism, humanistic or otherwise. In a sermon published nationally in 1949 he warned, "Man who has been worshipping himself since the Renaissance does not find it easy to worship God."[4] He went on to protest Swinburne's proud but misguided faith, "Glory to man in the highest, for man is the master of things." Penrose celebrates the intended and potential grandeur of "man" made in the image of God, but he reminds us of our awesome power to self-destruct. So qualified, Penrose may be said to be a "Renaissance man."

Penrose is both a generalist and specialist, as Shurden has cogently observed. He is a specialist in church history, with major interest in the modern period, with close attention to Baptist history, and yet further concentration upon Baptists in the American scene. But Penrose has never lived within the narrow bounds of a single field. He does not fit the image of the scholar content to know "more and more about less and less." Emphatically, he is *not* "a jack of all trades and a master of none." He can function competently as a specialist in many fields.

Penrose's published works reflect a "Renaissance man's" wide-ranging interests and knowledge: history, theology, philosophy, psychology, novels, drama, poetry, music, art, and almost anything relating to the human scene. This is reflected in his insistence through the years upon a real liberal arts education for all college students, protesting its erosion since World War II. Two recent examples may be cited: his H. I. Hester Lectures delivered in 1984 before the Association of Southern Baptist Colleges,[5] and his address at the inauguration of W. Morgan Patterson as President of Georgetown College.[6]

Versatility and wide-ranging interests were apparent already in college years. Penrose played the violin for us and played it well. He sang in the choral club. He was on the debating team. He played freshman football, all 139 pounds of him! He participated in weekend mission trips with the Volunteer Band, and his talks in the churches excited his peers for their range, cogency, and eloquence. Already, there were the buddings of the "Renaissance man."

In college, Penrose completed three majors: history, education, and English. Among the fields in which he has the competence of a specialist is English literature. A sample of his ability to draw upon this area, selected almost

---

[4] "Christian Faith Confronts the Modern Mind," *Best Sermons* 1949–50 Edition, ed. G. Paul Butler (New York: Harper & Brothers, 1949) 130f. This was one of fifty-two sermons selected from 6,585 submitted.

[5] *The Southern Baptist Educator* 48:6 (July-August 1984).

[6] "Called to Serve, Called to Lead," Addresses and Prayer on the occasion of the inauguration of Dr. Morgan Patterson, Georgetown College, 22 October 1984. No pagination.

at random, appears in an article on theological students, at one point of which he dealt with the pursuit of relevance:

> Those who prize secularity highly would be inclined to interpret relevance to mean relevance to the traditional concerns and responsibilities of the church. And yet the search for relevance is also pursued by those engaged in a profound search for the meaning of the gospel at a time when the abyss of meaninglessness is always near the edge of our common life. These are their questions: What does the Christian gospel have to offer those such as Albert Camus, who find life basically absurd? What does the Christian faith have to say to those who, with Tennessee Williams, believe that man is imprisoned in an impenetrable loneliness? What does the church have to contribute to those like J. D. Salinger, who are deeply disturbed by the phonies in our status-conscious society? What does the preacher have to say to those like Eugene O'Neill, for whom reality without illusions is unbearable? What can the minister contribute to modern man committed to his idols of success, sex, and security—idols which he alternately trusts and doubts?[7]

Supportive of this perception of Penrose as a generalist is my memory of a momentous decision he made when we were young professors in New Orleans. He began there as instructor in theology (1943–45), then became associate professor in church history and theology (1945–48), next professor of church history and theology (1948–51), and then professor of church history (1951–59). As the Seminary grew, a decision was made to create two distinct departments, Church History and Systematic Theology. Penrose was given the option of heading either department. He made the difficult decision, opting for church history, although his interests were about as deep in one field as the other and his credentials excellent for either. Why did Penrose choose church history over theology? One answer is that probably more interests can be subsumed under the umbrella of history than theology. As historian, Penrose could be theologian also, and more.

PENROSE AS COMMUNICATOR

A key to understanding Penrose St. Amant is his mind with its power to become informed, to understand, and to articulate. Gathering facts is no small achievement in itself, but Penrose as a historian is more than a computerized data bank. The facts cannot be interpreted unless they are known, but the real task is in knowing how to assess them in terms of meaning, causal factors, and consequences. Penrose has that gift. As minister and historian, communication is primary; and much of his genius is here. His students have often attested to his power of communicating. Anyone who says, "I understand it

---

[7]"The Private World of Theological Students," *Religion in Life* 31:4 (Autumn 1962): 501.

but cannot explain it" probably does not understand it. Seeing it and saying it belong together, and so it is with Penrose.

A sample of Penrose's power to distinguish things which differ, penetrate to the heart of the matter, and say it with compelling clarity appears in an article which, among other things, deals with theological relevance:

> Relevance can mean conformity as well as creative engagement. It can mean acculturation in the sense of compromise with the dominant values of a culture as well as creative confrontation of the culture with the claims of Christ. Serious theological students who rightly seek to distinguish between Christ and culture sometimes fail to realize that the church is inevitably secularized to some degree in any society in which it survives. A socially effective idea must be institutionalized and thus in some measure acculturated. Young prophets find it difficult to be organization men and thus to labor in the context of religious institutions. And yet this is in some measure essential.[8]

Again, "Vitality without structure is like a rushing stream which overflows its banks and dissipates itself by seeking to go everywhere at once, and thus loses both depth and direction."[9]

As a communicator, Penrose is both writer and speaker. He developed earlier as lecturer, and then discovered the joy and challenge of the pulpit as well as the lectern. He is highly effective in each of these media.

If, indeed, Penrose is a generalist as well as a specialist, that fact may bear upon his ministry of writing. A question sometimes asked by friends and followers is, "Why has Penrose not written more?" The question is a proper one, as Penrose himself would agree. The answer is not a simple one, but there are clues both to the range and limits of his writings.

To begin with, Penrose has actually written extensively, more than appears when one looks for books alone. His writings are considerable, scattered among many publications: chapters in books, articles in professional journals, periodic literature, academic lectures, sermons, and some books.[10] Massive tomes have an important place in scholarship, and it is to just such scholars as Penrose St. Amant that we look for such works, often serving as definitive summations or programmatic breakthroughs. Not to be underestimated is the catalytic power of an article, a lecture, or a sermon for understanding the past or present or for showing the way ahead. With due respect for the tome, sometimes there is more light in an essay or lecture than in a heavy book. A part of the genius Penrose has is his ability to pack much into a little space.[11] In addition to some books, Penrose has covered in articles a

---

[8] Ibid.
[9] Ibid.
[10] See in this issue, Lynn E. May, Jr., "C. Penrose St. Amant: A Bibliography."
[11] For example see "Communicating the Gospel in the Eighties," 61–72.

wide range of subjects, many by request. Writing on so wide a range of subjects is better suited to articles than books.

Two motivations may bear upon any scholar's disposition to write or not write: "publish or perish" and "publish and perish." Unfortunately, the latter has been more of a threat than the former for Southern Baptists, from Toy and Whitsitt to Clark and Elliott. It is doubtful that either motive or threat would be decisive for Penrose. He has no apparent security needs compelling him to write or not write. He appears to be sufficiently at peace with himself to be free from either compulsion. He is sufficiently secure and motivated to write what he feels important to write, and he is realist enough to sense what has the promise of being productive. His balanced judgment and sense of direction are reflected in an interview with *The Theological Educator*:

> I often tell my students to choose their battles and not to escalate every skirmish into a major conflict. In some situations, half a loaf is better than none. But there are other situations where, regardless of the cost, one takes a stand and pays the price.[12]

Although an excellent writer, Penrose possibly is even a better speaker, whether at the lectern or pulpit; for in speaking his whole person enters more fully into the act of communicating: voice, face, gestures, pause, the sharp focus, the sudden outburst. Although he practices the scholar's objectivity, he never speaks or writes merely as a spectator. In the best sense of the term, Penrose is a partisan. Scholarship for him is not all search; it also is finding. Ministry for him is not just reporting; it is commitment. Behind his writings is the whole person; but it is in teaching and preaching that many see him best approach his potential.

With such gifts in speech and writing, one may ask why Penrose devoted precious years to administration, Dean of the School of Theology at Southern Seminary and President of the international Baptist Seminary in Rüschlikon. Of course, the answer most readily at hand is the sense of divine direction. But how is this sensed apart from one's gifts, disposition, and commitment? Two specifics are suggested: concern for what is sought in theological education and the gifts for bringing people together, respecting their diversities and maximizing their commonalities. He has the temperament and expertise to work in a pluralistic community, in particular academic ones with their gifted "prima donnas," bringing them together as a team without undue encroachment upon their individual identities. Thus administration for him has not been a radical departure from motives expressed through lectern and pulpit.

In this connection, it is remarkable that Penrose has been at the center of several seminaries without himself having been the center of controversy. It

---

[12]"An Interview with Penrose St. Amant," *The Theological Educator* 12:2 (Spring 1982): 25.

is not that he has been neutral or silent. In part probably is his distaste for controversy. If the issue is important to him, he will listen to the other person and also have his say, clearly and concisely, leaving it there if necessary with his characteristic, "And that's that." He will not be coerced, and neither has he any disposition to coerce.

But there is more. This aversion to controversy relates in part to Penrose as a private person as well as a public servant. He is committed to responsible churchmanship, and he enjoys the company of friends; but he also requires a measure of privacy. Penrose is not a possessive person or a combatant who defends his own "turf." He is a private person who requires his own space. He respects the privacy of others; he requires it for himself. He spoke to this effect in an unpublished chapel message at Southern Seminary (8 January 1980), "If I were a Seminary Student Again." He said, "In controversial matters, St. Amant I would choose my battles . . . I would cultivate the art of accommodation, realizing that leadership is frequently the art of the possible." Further, "I would preserve a private life in the midst of my public life."

In his inaugural address as dean at Southern Seminary twenty years earlier, Penrose made clear his commitment to "educate for participation . . . leaders who think and act courageously and creatively, leaders who have basic respect for thought and who are willing to run the risks of action."[13] To him, education is for understanding, for living, for action, and not for private security. But there is more. For Penrose, controversy is not a goal or something for its own sake. Honest inquiry and open debate point properly to the harnessing of diverse resources in community. He spoke thus of educational administration as "the art of the possible":

> If this is taken to mean a kind of accommodation based upon expediency, then, this is a counsel of cowardice. However, if this is taken to mean the highest possible resolutions of honest differences of opinion in a competent and dedicated community and if it is assumed that responsible leadership is involved, leadership that keeps the institution moving out of its historic past to an increasing creative future, then this is a counsel of wisdom.[14]

Penrose has the commitment and courage to "purge distorted and accidental elements" from our heritage but also the disposition to "share joyfully in the heritage which nurtures us."[15] He is more irenic and constructive than combative, as reflected in this probing:

> And who is my neighbor? My neighbor is humanity—the humanity I confront day by day in my task, in my memory, in my imagination. My neigh-

---

[13] "Theological Education and the Denominational Seminary," *Review and Expositor,* Special Inaugural Supplement 57:2 (April 1960): 255.
[14] Ibid., 250.
[15] Ibid., 243.

bor is my friend, who sustains me, and also the one who, for whatever reason, is suspicious and fearful of me. He is the one who is near and the one who is far. He is my student, my teacher, my colleague. He is the lonely and hopeless one whether he lives in a hovel or a mansion. Let us seize this sensitive concern 'we dimly recognize in our purer moments' and sustain it in our lives. Thus the prison of self-love is broken, anxieties are tempered, and we can enter creatively into the lives of others in the daily round. It is relatively easy to be heroic in a crisis but the real test comes in routine tasks.[16]

Possibly out of this complexity of aversion to controversy, disposition to privacy, bold creativity, irenic constructiveness, and responsible leadership, Penrose has sensed the time to speak and the time to be silent, the time to write and the time not to write. He has said enough and written enough to keep us busy, if we are open to it.

TRIBUTE FROM A STUDENT

The lines below were written by Don B. Harbuck, one of the finest students ever to sit in anyone's classes. His tribute to Penrose says it better than others of us, try as we may. As Penrose would say, Don's death left our world with less light, but his witness lives on.

PENROSE ST. AMANT

A strange sort of saint
  this St. Amant!
Suave and secular
  with irreverent hair
  and clothes reckless to fashion
    laughter unrestrained
    rage uncensored
    kindness unexpected.

A holy man incognito
  awakening the within
  summoning the beyond
  hallowing the earth
  evoking harmony
    from the debris of history.

He shocked us gently with those
    shrines—
  the Quarter and the Shack
    and the Stage
    and the Mazes of man's journey.

---

[16]Ibid., 240f.

AN INTERPRETATION OF THE MAN

Hearing the Voice
  in theatres and Luther
  in novels and Niebuhr,
For him
  the Cross never lost
    its scandal and glory
  nor faith
    its prodigal paradox.
  God remained always
    God the Father
      never quite a Friend.

Profiled pensively against the chalkboard
  lost in vision
  eyes fixed fleetingly
    beyond the class
    on some hidden horizon
He scouted unsettled frontiers
  for us
  his pilgrim company
Left shaken by
  his assaults on our assurance
    his affection for our foes
      his appetite for our future.

What haunted and hurt him was our healing—
  beckoning roads untaken
  inviting searches unmade
  gestating books undelivered.
He laid down his life
          in rocky soil
       on two continents
    out of love's necessity
  with the irrational logic of sacrifice
For us his people
  who kill our saints
    by calling everyone a saint
And with our saints
  have slain now our senses
    until another season returns
In mercy
  from the furrowed graves
    of our forsaken saints.

Don B. Harbuck
August 1980

C. PENROSE ST. AMANT: TEACHER AND HISTORIAN

CLAUDE HOWE
New Orleans Baptist Theological Seminary, New Orleans LA 70126

Modern historians admit that complete objectivity is impossible. Interpreters of history bring a frame of reference or point of view to their materials that is never totally overcome. Recognition of this limitation assists the interpreter from allowing the frame of reference to create conclusions not justified by the sources and warns that the particular interpretation is never absolutely definitive.

Even if this historian could be totally objective about persons and events of the ancient past, he could not be in interpreting and evaluating Penrose St. Amant as teacher and historian. Thirty years ago the present writer, inspired more by the teacher than the subject, began a serious study of church history under the direction of Professor St. Amant. The student attended virtually every class taught by the professor for the next two years, served as his graduate fellow, absorbed his understanding of historical developments and principles, and shared a friendship that has continued for three decades.

Two typical events come to mind that illustrate the openness to and interest in students by Penrose St. Amant. Early in this student's graduate program, the professor invited him to a lovely home in the historic French Quarter of New Orleans, made accessible any books needed from a massive personal library, and often transported books back and forth that were borrowed. More recently, after thirty years, the professor called the former student unexpectedly and informed him that two tickets to the NCAA final four college basketball tournament in New Orleans were available if desired. These matters are recorded not because they are unique but because they are representative of the relationship established by Professor St. Amant with dozens of college and seminary teachers and denominational leaders who studied under him during four decades of teaching at Southern Baptist seminaries.

St. Amant recognized that excellent teaching requires intensive preparation. He graduated from Louisiana College in 1936 and received the master of arts degree from Louisiana State University the next year. Master (1940) and doctor (1942) of theology degrees were earned at the New Orleans Baptist Theological Seminary. The dissertation for the latter degree program was entitled "Some Gnostic Influences on Early Christian Thought."

After completing his basic theological training, St. Amant taught for one year at Hannibal-LaGrange College in Missouri and then returned to his alma mater, New Orleans Seminary. His academic preparation continued with several summers of study at Union Theological Seminary in New York and at Columbia University. His first sabbatical leave was spent at Edinburgh University, from which he received the Ph.D. in 1952. His dissertation there was entitled "The Rise and Early Development of the Princeton School of Theology."

St. Amant culminated sixteen years (1943-59) of classroom teaching at the New Orleans Seminary in 1959, becoming at that time professor of church history and Dean of the School of Theology at Southern Baptist Theological Seminary. A distinguished career as dean (1959-69) and professor (1959-72) at Southern was followed by the presidency of the international Baptist Seminary at Rüschlikon, Switzerland, for five years (1972-77). He then "retired," or rather returned to what he loved most, classroom teaching, and virtually without a break has spent the past decade teaching at Golden Gate, Southwestern, and Southern Seminaries, and Louisiana College.

A consideration of St. Amant as teacher and historian is a single task, not a dual one. The teacher is a perceptive historian and the historian a sensitive teacher. Classroom instruction and written interpretation may be discussed separately but reflect the same person and vocation. The classroom provides the major focus for the first topic considered below and the manuscript for the other three but the desire is that they complement rather than compartmentalize. The teacher-historian will be considered as teacher of Christian history, theologian of Christian faith, historian of Christian institutions, and interpreter of Christian values.

TEACHER OF CHRISTIAN HISTORY

Penrose St. Amant is a teacher of Christian history. He debates as do other scholars whether church history or Christian history is a more appropriate title for courses describing the historical development of the followers of Christ, but the content of his courses focuses on the Christian movement in the broadest sense. Protestant sympathies are not hidden, but they do not require polemical attacks on Roman Catholicism; Baptist convictions are evident, but they do not relegate other believers to second class status. He finds appropriate the counsel of T. S. Eliot to live and think in "Christian categories," the heart of which is to love God and neighbor fully and freely.[1]

The teacher does not allow his students to forget that Christian history is history. The rigorous standards of the historical discipline are not relaxed but reinforced when the subject matter studied is a segment of Christian development. Authenticity and credibility of sources, rigor in logical deductions, monitoring of bias, awareness of limitations, contributions of other disciplines, and similar concerns are as important for Christian history as secular history. The "continuities and contingencies" of life are better understood

---

[1] Penrose St. Amant, "Theological Education and the Denominational Seminary," *Review and Expositor* 62:2 (April 1960): 240.

through historical study, and historical understanding provides inspiration as well as information.[2]

Whatever the subject or specialty within it, Penrose St. Amant first and foremost functions as a teacher. Some teachers parade their knowledge for the world to admire and others pose as an authority on virtually everything, sharing their wisdom liberally. Students are impressed by the sheer brilliance and extensive knowledge of Professor St. Amant in a different way, by his humble invitation to a pilgrimage of learning about matters that are really important today as in the past. "History is more than a description of what is finished," he notes frequently. "It can easily be corrupted for partisan purposes, but it can be a resource for the present and a guide for the future."[3]

From time to time Professor St. Amant utilized a film (Martin Luther) or visiting guest speakers (Contemporary American Religion), but his normal teaching methodology was to lecture. Students remember many sessions when he entered the classroom lecturing and departed in the same manner. His modest reply that this discouraged students from asking questions convinced no one, for discussion of questions raised by students or the professor provided keen insights into how historical events relate to contemporary issues. Taking of notes was often difficult because of the extensive amount of material shared and the vast range of ideas incorporated, but more important than recording factual knowledge was the broadening perspective gained from a keen mind grappling with great issues of the past and present. Literature and theology, television and psychology, obscure documents and contemporary newspapers provided sources for lecture, discussion, or writing. What classes lacked in pedantic organization were rewarded by perpetual interest, for a French flair for the dramatic insured that interaction with past events was never dull or irrelevant.

Many former students now serving in responsible positions recall a variety of impressions about St. Amant as teacher. "I knew him as friend of students, one who wanted to relate to us, to challenge us, and to inspire us," recalled one. "He was a man of integrity, of truth, of spiritual depth, of intellectual honesty. And he treated his students with respect," commented another. "Little things come to mind—the way he added Louisiana Hot Sauce to practically everything he ate, his eclectic mind which introduced his students to new areas of thought, the way he arranged for a TV set to be in the seminar room when the World Series was being played." One recollected that "he sometimes seemed annoyed with mediocrity and once dismissed a seminar in its early minutes because the student presenting a paper had done poor preparation." Perhaps one student summarized the matter by stating that "St.

---

[2]St. Amant, "Southern Baptists: Unity in Diversity," *Baptist History and Heritage* 7 (January 1972): 21.

[3]Ibid.

Amant is for me a good model of one who cherishes the best of our Baptist heritage, demonstrates great appreciation for Christians of all denominations, and calls us Baptists to continuous self-examination under the searchlight of scripture." An open mind and an open Bible, as Professor St. Amant often recommended, but this did not mean an empty mind or a legalistic Bible.[4]

THEOLOGIAN OF CHRISTIAN FAITH

St. Amant taught theology along with history and insisted that a competent theologian must be a knowledgeable historian. The Holland Lectures delivered at Southwestern (1954) and repeated as the Layne Lectures at New Orleans (1955) were entitled "Christian Faith and History." Printed in limited editions but not published, these lectures pursued a fundamental thesis that "history is an insoluble enigma without Christian presuppositions and that the Christian faith cannot be understood unless its historical character is recognized."[5] Four lectures focused upon Christian faith and historical understanding, historical forms, modern western culture, and the modern mind. They reflect St. Amant at his best as historian and theologian, philosopher and preacher, scholar and Christian.

A brief introduction indicates that "man's insatiable curiosity" to know more about the past, present, and future justifies the study of history in general and church history in particular.[6] History is significant for understanding Christian faith, and Christian faith is essential for properly understanding history. Study of history should make one aware of the conditioned character of Christianity and assist in distinguishing the permanent from the passing. But efforts by "scientific" historians to describe what happened through an objective analysis of sources, though commendable, was held by him to be limited in value.

Christian faith provides a perspective that includes meaning, namely that God has revealed himself in a particular history and through this revelation effects salvation. "The Christian faith that God has disclosed himself in a holy history in Jesus Christ for our redemption is 'foolishness' to those who believe in the sovereignty of nature or reason," St. Amant concluded, "but is 'wisdom' to those who, in the famous words of Blaise Pascal, believe in 'the God of Abraham, the God of Isaac, the God of Jacob, not of the philosophers and the scholars.'"[7]

In discussing Christian faith and historical understanding Professor St. Amant elaborates further upon the significance of history for the Christian

---

[4]The above citations are from a private collection of letters in the possession of the author.

[5]St. Amant. "Christian Faith and History" (Layne Lectures, New Orleans Baptist Theological Seminary, 1955) 3.

[6]Ibid., 5.

[7]Ibid., 8–9.

faith and then addresses how various Christian groups respond to the concept of the relativity of historical knowledge. If history is the primary sphere in which God reveals himself, then how does one respond to assertions about the relativity of historical knowledge?

Nature and experience are not devoid of all knowledge of God, as Karl Barth argues, but natural theology and religious or moral experience are "subsidiary sources" alongside the revelation of the eternal God through mighty acts in history.[8] "Christian faith affirms the normative value of a particular historical process and a particular person who is its climax."[9] The "simultaneity and successiveness" of which Baron Friedrich von Hügel spoke, between our temporal life and God's eternal life, has come.[10] "God himself has bridged the wide ditch, using human history as an instrument. The eternal God entered time in Jesus Christ."[11] Christianity is a historical religion because the revelation that underlies it is a historical revelation.

Christian faith not only is grounded upon a historical revelation but is also a historical movement that has assumed a variety of forms. "The Christian faith possesses unique features adequately accounted for only in terms of revelation but these unique features have been historically mediated and sometimes terribly obscured and distorted in the ongoing process of history."[12] But does acknowledging relativity require abandoning all absolutes and adopting skepticism, or absolutizing a relative and manifesting fanaticism. These and other responses have been evident in various schools of theological thought.

Roman Catholics respond to the problem by affirming an infallible church, which is "a form of idolatry on the religious level."[13] Liberal Protestants stress the historical Jesus and religious experience. "This is untenable because the historical Jesus is not really historical and religious experience is sometimes not really religious."[14] Modernists and humanists accommodate to relativity and stress some religious feature such as love or a vague humanitarianism. Neo-protestantism centers in biblical faith, interpreted in terms of Reformation theology, but relies too heavily upon paradox and a few classical theologians.

Christianity and culture sustain a reciprocal relationship, each leaving impressions upon the other, as Kenneth Scott Latourette has demonstrated clearly. But to say that Christian faith has been historically mediated does not mean that it can be totally accounted for as a result of purely historical forces.

---

[8]Ibid., 12.
[9]Ibid., 19.
[10]Ibid., 18.
[11]Ibid., 19.
[12]Ibid., 23.
[13]Ibid., 42.
[14]Ibid.

Acknowledging relativity does not require abandoning all absolutes. "There are permanent elements in the Christian faith that come out of a Divine revelation," St. Amant observed, "but these perennial features must be expressed in the changing categories of the cultures and communities in which this faith is expressed. This is the crux of the problem of Christian faith and history."[15] This lecture is concluded by the professor with a dual appeal. "Let us reaffirm our biblical faith in a world that is drifting either without faith or gripped by false faiths," he said.[16] "Let us reaffirm our freedom in a world where demagogues, political and religious, set themselves up as arbiters of human destiny, superimposing upon the minds and consciences of men a bondage more deadly than any concentration camp."[17]

In addressing Christian faith and its historical forms, Professor St. Amant identifies eight major problems or crises faced by the developing Christian movement across the centuries and indicates some ways that these have conditioned the faith. The Jewish-Christian conflict broke the power of a narrow nationalism and sustained a universal outlook based on divine grace. Gnosticism hastened the development of the Old Catholic Church defined in terms of organization, doctrine, and literary authority. Encounters with Greek mystery cults may have encouraged sacramental tendencies. Controversy over the person of Jesus Christ leading to and beyond the Nicene Council made Jesus a remote theological figure and elevated the incarnation more than the atonement but protected his role in God's redemptive and revelatory activity.

A faith already partially obscured by hellenization was further conditioned with the rise of the imperial state church under Constantine by involving it in the political problems of the Roman Empire. The shattering of this Empire by the Germanic tribes made the Catholic Church the unifying force in the West. Priestly and feudal forces were wedded, and soon this conditioned community unreservedly identified itself with the Kingdom of God. The Protestant Reformation challenged many of these developments, insisting upon individual access to God and upon the authority of Scripture over popes or councils, but many departures from biblical faith were retained. Both Protestants and Catholics have been challenged by the rise of modern science and philosophy and this challenge continues to the present time.

At every point in these developments, Christian faith has been conditioned by historical circumstances and has struggled with what is permanent and what is passing, as it does today. The desire to be relevant pushes the faith toward secularism and the desire to be unique pushes it toward sectarianism. "We must seek to relate creatively both of these dimensions-the dimension of relevance and the dimension of uniqueness," St. Amant stated.

---

[15]Ibid., 26.
[16]Ibid., 42.
[17]Ibid., 42–43.

"The uniqueness of the Christian faith must not be a cloak of self-righteousness with which we shut out the troubled world," he continued, "but an instrument of redemption which we bring to bear upon this lost generation."[18]

St. Amant regards western culture as "essentially the culture of Greece, inherited from the Greeks by the Romans, transfused with Christianity, and enlarged by countless men and movements until our own time."[19] The Christian faith has been significant in western culture but in the modern period this culture "owes more to the Renaissance than the Reformation and is more classical than Christian, though some Greek elements have been altered and deepened by Christian insights."[20]

Man, for example, is a more towering and tragic figure than modern theories, drawn from the Greeks through the Renaissance, conceive him to be. These theories underestimate his stature and overestimate his virtue. His uniqueness derives from God, but his very transcendence over nature or reason also becomes the source of his sin. History, likewise, must not be viewed in terms of inevitable progress without regard for divine grace, for historical development may include a destructive aspect. Scientific growth, for example, brings both healing and destruction. "Modern Culture, with its incredible technological achievements, nevertheless wavers between utopianism and disillusionment."[21] Christian faith, with a profound realism anchored in God, recognizes both our potentialities and our problems, and so "enables us to assume our responsibilities without illusion and yet with triumphant hope."[22]

Discussing Christian faith and the modern mind at mid-century, St. Amant saw a "crisis of faiths"[23] with rising interest in religion accompanied by much despair. Intellectuals and the educational system still viewed science and the scientific method as the hope of the future. "Thus the modern mind with which the Christian faith must come to grips is immersed in a naturalistic philosophy which casts doubt upon ultimate value and truth."[24] Everything is relative except the scientific viewpoint. This has resulted in a tentativeness which enervates belief in human freedom and responsibility. "It is a faith which reduces man and his civilization to the level of mechanisms in order to understand them. It casts doubt upon life's most significant values," he argued, "and leaves man alone with his illusions in an essentially meaningless world. It is a faith which begins with the high hope that science is the key to our deepest problems and then it turns at last to despair."[25]

---

[18]Ibid., 72–73.
[19]Ibid., 74.
[20]Ibid.
[21]Ibid., 95.
[22]Ibid., 116.
[23]Ibid., 130.
[24]Ibid., 145.
[25]Ibid., 145–46.

The Christian faith accepts genuine achievements of science but does not regard them as ultimate. It understands not only man's plight but has a unique conception of the cure. "The solution to man's perennial problem is not a critical intelligence primarily, not social revolution, nor psychotherapy, but Divine redemption. Nothing less than the Divine invasion embodied in the Gospel is sufficient for our great need."[26]

These lectures have been summarized at some length because they reflect so many of the central concerns of Professor St. Amant. What is not as evident through a summary is the constant interaction with contemporary thinkers and literature. Catholic and Protestant, liberal and conservative, Christian and secularist are cited with approval or criticism. Although he could critique them both, Reinhold and Richard Niebuhr emerge as significant mentors, and scripture provides insight on all crucial issues.

No doubt some points would be revised today, but the central convictions would remain the same. In a recent interview (1982) he affirmed the authority of scripture, stressed the majesty and mystery of God, and criticized contemporary relativism and pluralism which often lead to skepticism or authoritarianism.[27] "The contemporary world, therefore, is ripe for the proliferation of cults, the resurgence of fundamentalism, and a renewed liberalism, all of which offer simplistic solutions to the complicated problems of today's world."[28] The response of Christian faith must be in terms of the gospel revealed in Christ and recorded in scripture. "Divine revelation is the self-disclosure of God in history and supremely in the life of a man, not a divine magician, not a theophany. God came in Jesus as completely as he could possibly come in a genuine human life."[29] The gospel requires justice and love, righteousness and grace, demand and forgiveness, revealing a priestly task for the hurt in the world and a prophetic task where there is injustice. The gospel judges all self-righteousness and idolatry but offers meaning and hope for those who are open to receive it.

HISTORIAN OF CHRISTIAN INSTITUTIONS

St. Amant could be described accurately more as a historian of ideas than institutions. The broad sweep of Christian, western, human developments provided a vast resource for setting forth a perspective that was historical and personal and Christian. But the professor could also function as researcher and narrator for events regional and denominational. Two books that focus on Christian groups in Louisiana are in the latter category, namely *A Short*

---

[26]Ibid., 165.

[27]St. Amant, "Southern Baptist Theology Today: An Interview," *The Theological Educator* 12:2 (Spring 1982): 16–31.

[28]Ibid., 21.

[29]Ibid., 22.

History of Louisiana Baptists (1948) and *A History of the Presbyterian Church in Louisiana* (1961).

Both books were written by invitation, the first of the Centennial Committee of the Louisiana Baptist Convention and the second of the trustees for Presbyterian publications for the Synod of Louisiana. The Committee "unanimously"[30] selected the professor and the trustees recorded that "a trained historian, a capable writer, a man of great knowledge and broad sympathies, he was ideally suited to record the history of the Presbyterians of Louisiana."[31] St. Amant indicated that friends described him as half-Presbyterian and half-Baptist. "Strictly speaking, that is not correct. I am a convinced Baptist but my Baptist faith has been enlarged and deepened by this unique contact with the Presbyterians."[32]

Both books though written for popular or general audiences were thoroughly researched from primary sources. The Baptist history, however, contains no documentation and a brief bibliography. The Presbyterian history contains extensive documentation (thirty-six pages) and an excellent bibliography (eight pages) of primary and secondary sources. More attention is given in the Baptist history to the general background of Louisiana, but both address problems faced by Protestant groups in a dominant Catholic culture, especially in south Louisiana.

A focus upon prominent personalities and events makes the Presbyterian history much more readable, as does the basic format in print and style. Both show the close connections with similar groups in Mississippi, and each documents organizational developments toward state bodies, whether Convention or Synod. Both trace educational, benevolent, and missionary advances and give due emphasis to controversies and divisions.

Neither volume is triumphal in tone but both reflect gratitude and respect for the heritage transmitted. The Baptist story "started unpropitiously with small and scattered groups of courageous men and women who, having subdued the wilderness and built with their hands crude frontier cabins and churches, gradually developed a distinctive culture and achieved a unity of purpose and policy which embraced the entire state."[33] Baptist growth far exceeded that of Presbyterian, but impact upon culture cannot be calculated only in quantitative terms. Presbyterian gifts have been in the realm of moral and spiritual values and their heritage is one of courage and sacrifice. "Let those who make up its churches and homes, those who give themselves gladly as

---

[30]St. Amant, *A Short History of Louisiana Baptists* (Nashville: Broadman Press, 1948) Foreword.

[31]St. Amant, *A History of the Presbyterian Church in Louisiana* (Richmond VA.: Whittet and Shepperson, 1961) 7.

[32]Ibid., 10.

[33]*Louisiana Baptists*, Introduction.

deacons and elders, those who occupy the sacred desks, those who seek in office, shop, and countryside to be faithful to its precepts,'' concluded the Baptist historian in assessing Louisiana Presbyterians, ''draw strength from this noble past for the 'grand and awful time' which lies before us today and tomorrow.''[34]

St. Amant in his student days served as president of the Louisiana Baptist Student Union (1934-35) and maintained an interest and involvement in student work across the years. He published a *Historical Sketch of the Louisiana Baptist Student Union* (1956) that briefly described the background, beginnings, and growth of the Union in the state and at each college.[35] His native state remained a focus of analysis in an essay entitled ''Louisiana'' for *Religion in the Southern States* edited by Samuel S. Hill (1983). This essay described differences in religion and culture between predominantly Roman Catholic south Louisiana and mostly Protestant north Louisiana. St. Amant then sketched the development of various religious groups in Louisiana including Roman Catholics, Episcopalians, Presbyterians, Baptists, Methodists, Disciples, Lutherans, Mennonites, Pentecostals, Jews, and adherents of Voodooism.[36]

Both the Historical Commission and Historical Society of the Southern Baptist Convention have been productive in collecting and publishing materials related to Baptists. St. Amant has been involved as participant, consultant, speaker, writer, and supporter of these activities throughout his career, and the present executive director of the Commission pursued doctoral work under his direction at New Orleans Seminary. *Baptist History and Heritage* and segments of *The Quarterly Review* published by the Commission contain many articles written by St. Amant. Additionally, he contributed an article entitled ''Other Baptist Bodies'' for *Baptist Advance* published jointly by the SBC and eight other Baptist groups (1964).[37] This article focused on Baptist bodies not involved in the joint venture. The Commission has also sponsored the publishing of the *Encyclopedia of Southern Baptists* in four volumes, two updating the initial two, and St. Amant has served as a consultant and writer for these volumes.[38]

Perhaps passing reference should be made here to the doctoral dissertations on Gnosticism and the Princeton theology written by St. Amant, if only

---

[34]*Presbyterian Church*, 246.

[35]St. Amant, *Historical Sketch of the Louisiana Baptist Student Union* (Department of Student Work, Louisiana Baptist Convention, 1956).

[36]St. Amant, ''Louisiana,'' in Samuel S. Hill, ed., *Religion in the Southern States: A Historical Study* (Macon GA.: Mercer University Press, 1983): 123–45.

[37]St. Amant, ''Other Baptist Bodies,'' in Davis Collier Woolley, ed., *Baptist Advance* (Nashville: Broadman Press, 1964) 368–84.

[38]See the *Encyclopedia of Southern Baptists* (Nashville: Broadman Press, 1958, 1971, 1982).

to register the diversity of interests and the influence of teachers who directed his studies.[39] The somewhat sketchy study of Gnosticism and the hefty analysis of Princeton theology were done at times when these topics were not central in historical interests as they later became. Professor E. F. Haight of New Orleans Seminary and Professor John Baillie of Edinburgh University were formative figures in guiding the academic development of Penrose St. Amant.

The range of interests continued as Professor St. Amant encouraged students to pursue studies of liberal theologians such as Shailer Mathews or William Newton Clarke and personally wrote biographical essays on individuals as diverse as Graham Greene[40] and Albert Camus[41] and his friend Frank Stagg.[42] Secular humanism as well as Southern Baptists was appropriate for historical analysis for the God of Christian faith was the God of the universe, and Christian faith provided understanding and meaning for an otherwise enigmatic past and perplexing future.[43]

INTERPRETER OF CHRISTIAN VALUES

A former student observed that St. Amant represents a healthy wedding of classical and Christian learning, bearing marks of both the Renaissance and the Reformation in him. The former is evidenced by his "openness, tolerance, critical mindedness, broad scope of knowledge, and appreciation of human culture"; the latter by his "strong appreciation of and commitment to biblical teaching as repristinated by Luther, Calvin, and other sixteenth century reformers."[44] Certainly his views of God and man and the universe reflect more of the latter and are shaped further by his own personal experience and Baptist heritage. But these views are couched in a concern for human culture in totality and how Christians should understand and adapt and change aspects of this culture today.

St. Amant defines culture as "the pattern of values by which communities define the meaning of their existence."[45] It is a constellation of inward

---

[39] See "Some Gnostic Influences on Early Christian Thought" (Th.D. diss., New Orleans Baptist Theological Seminary, 1942) and "The Rise and Early Development of the Princeton School of Theology" (Ph.D. diss., University of Edinburgh, 1952).

[40] St. Amant, "God Gets His Man: A Study of Graham Greene," *Perspectives in Religious Studies* 1:1 (Spring 1974): 52-58.

[41] St. Amant, "God, Man, and Redemption in the Writings of Albert Camus," *Review and Expositor* 61:3 (Summer 1964): 156-66.

[42] St. Amant, "A Continuing Pilgrimage: A Biographical Sketch of Frank Stagg," *The Theological Educator* 8:1 (Fall 1977): 15-36.

[43] See "Secular Humanism and the State," *Report from the Capital* 36:5 (May 1981); "Baptists in a Revolutionary Age," *Baptist History and Heritage* 7:3 (July 1972); "Reformation: Old and New," *Review and Expositor* 64:2 (Spring 1967); "Our Baptist Heritage and the Church," *Baptist History and Heritage* 2:2 (July 1967).

[44] Private collections of letters in the possession of the author.

[45] St. Amant, "Toward an Understanding of Culture," *Review and Expositor* 61:1 (Winter 1964): 500.

values of which civilization is the outward expression. He accepts Paul Tillich's observation that "religion is the substance of culture" and that "culture is the expression of religion."[46] His essay "Toward an Understanding of Culture" moves from defining to criticizing culture, especially in the modern period. It tends to be secular and scientific and nationalistic and relativistic, so the choice is to form a new Christian culture or accept a pagan one. "We must recover the cultural heritage of the Christian faith and communicate it to a sub-religious and neo-pagan world."[47]

An essay entitled "Southern Baptists and Southern Culture" describes recent, rapid changes in Southern culture and their possible impact upon Southern Baptists.[48] "Little historical study has been given to the evident interpenetration of Southern culture and Southern Baptist life."[49] Southern Baptists will be involved in these cultural changes. "The real issue is whether Southern Baptists will try to hold a line that exists in the past or, what would be worse, will degenerate into a thoroughgoing culture-religion uncritically affirming current values," St. Amant warned, "or will assert with courage and enthusiasm a new and joyous breakthrough of evangelical faith sustaining a disciplined witness to the Kingdom of God which came with Christ."[50]

An article written in connection with the National Bicentennial shifted from a region to the entire nation and assessed "The Impact of Religion on the Shaping of American Values."[51] Protestant religion in general and Puritanism in particular shaped the value system of many Americans. Attitudes toward work and leisure, national destiny and moral concern, religious freedom and democratic institutions are rooted in religious faith. "The wisdom we need at this Bicentennial of our country is a gift of grace," Professor St. Amant concluded, "which could enable us to rise above both sentimentality and despair and could give us a prophetic vision of the future of ourselves and the world."[52]

If St. Amant is a blending of the Renaissance and the Reformation, then one should not be surprised at his continuing interest in education and communication. His voice and pen repeatedly stressed the value of a liberal arts education in colleges and universities and support and understanding for the

---

[46]Ibid.

[47]Ibid., 503.

[48]St. Amant, "Southern Baptists and Southern Culture," *Review and Expositor* 67:2 (Spring 1970): 141–52.

[49]Ibid., 145.

[50]Ibid., 151.

[51]St. Amant, "The Impact of Religion on the Shaping of American Values," *Review and Expositor* 73:1 (Winter 1976): 59–73.

[52]Ibid., 73.

public school system.⁵³ The role of theological education and the task of communicating the gospel in a post-modern world were too important to neglect very long and always were addressed with a cautious optimism.⁵⁴ "As Christians, our orientation is always toward hope. Our faith is rooted in the past, but it faces the future. It is open toward experimentation, toward 'a new heaven and a new earth'; not toward a static world," he said. "It is this quality of vision, the ability to dream, and to give substance to the dream, that has sent Christianity into the varied cultures of the world."⁵⁵

CONCLUSION

Clement of Alexandria described the impact of his teacher Pantaenus on him late in the second century. Clement had travelled widely and read extensively before arriving in Alexandria. There he abandoned further search, for in Pantaenus he found "a truly Sicilian bee" who "drew honey from the flowers in the meadow of the apostles and prophets, and implanted in the souls of his pupils pure knowledge."⁵⁶ Many students have found in Penrose St. Amant "a truly Sicilian bee" and have learned from him the developments and meaning of Christian history.

---

⁵³St. Amant, "Baptists and Public Education: An Historical Perspective," *The Quarterly Review* 44:2 (January 1984): 66–78; "New Directions in Baptist Colleges and Universities," *Review and Expositor* 64:1 (Winter 1967): 41–47.

⁵⁴St. Amant, "Communicating the Gospel in the Eighties," *The Quarterly Review* 41:3 (April 1981): 61–72.

⁵⁵Ibid., 72.

⁵⁶James Ernest Leonard Oulton and Henry Chadwick, editors and translators, *Alexandrian Christianity*, vol. 2 of *The Library of Christian Classics* (Philadelphia: The Westminster Press) 16.

C. PENROSE ST. AMANT: DEAN AT SOUTHERN, 1959—1969

E. GLENN HINSON
The Southern Baptist Theological Seminary, Louisville KY 40280

Penrose St. Amant served as Dean of the School of Theology at The Southern Baptist Theological Seminary during one of the institution's most traumatic periods since the era immediately after the Civil War. In 1958 the Board of Trustees had dismissed thirteen members of the faculty of the School of Theology after a prolonged administrative controversy with President Duke K. McCall.[1] When St. Amant came as dean, he faced the gargantuan tasks of rebuilding a depleted faculty, restoring confidence in the administration, easing tensions between faculty and administration, raising faculty morale, responding to notations by the accrediting agency, and, in general, getting the school moving forward once more as a major contributor to American theological education. In a decade he did a remarkable job on all counts.

AN INVITATION

St. Amant was not an obvious choice for the deanship. Although he and McCall had known one another for many years, St. Amant had not served in any administrative capacity either at Hannibal-Lagrange College in Missouri (1942–43) or at the Baptist Bible Institute in New Orleans, which became New Orleans Baptist Theological Seminary (1943–59). St. Amant's name, however, was suggested by Dale Moody, a member of the faculty, and the faculty responded warmly to the suggestion.[2] McCall had confidence in St. Amant, the first faculty member he employed when he became president of the Baptist Bible Institute and with whom he maintained a close personal friendship even after leaving New Orleans to become executive secretary of the Executive Committee of the Southern Baptist Convention.

Other considerations besides friendship doubtless contributed to McCall's invitation. The controverted situation at Southern argued for an outsider who could assess the problems in an objective way, as St. Amant proved he could do, and thus reduce suspicions and tensions which still lingered. Although St. Amant had not published a great deal by this time,[3] he possessed good academic credentials and reputation. More critically, both McCall and

---

[1]The controversy itself will not be discussed here. My analysis of it can be found in an article on "the Southern Baptist Theological Seminary" in *Encyclopedia of Southern Baptists*, vol. 3 (Nashville: Broadman Press, 1971: 1978–83.

[2]Phone interview with Duke K. McCall, 15 August 1988.

[3]See Lynn E. May, Jr., "C. Penrose St. Amant: A Bibliography," below.

members of the faculty felt comfortable with him, McCall by virtue of long association and the faculty by virtue of his being one of them.

Fairly lengthy negotiations indicate that St. Amant did not jump at the chance to become dean.[4] He liked New Orleans, both the city and the seminary, and was reluctant to leave as long as Roland Leavell remained as president. A close relationship with his aging father also held him back, as it had in 1937 when he considered where he would go to obtain his theological education. Moreover, he felt that teaching rather than administration was his vocation and knew the situation at Southern well enough to proceed with caution.

In his negotiations with the president and trustees St. Amant insisted on clarity vis-a-vis the role of the dean. He impressed on the trustees the need for the dean to control the initiative in faculty acquisitions. In a letter to Cort R. Flint, a trustee from South Carolina, dated 12 May 1959, he wrote,

> I feel that it should be made clear that the dean of the School of Theology should be able to take initiative in acquiring new faculty member (*sic*), and I feel that this should be definitely stated in the policy of faculty acquisitions that will be adopted by the Board at its next meeting. I fully recognize both the right and the responsibility of the faculty at this point but the dean's hands should not be tied.[5]

In the same letter he also asked that the trustees make clear that the dean would be present in board meetings where his recommendations were presented, eventually chair meetings of the Dean's Council, be able to appoint an assistant dean if he felt the need for it, and assume complete responsibility for dealing with the American Association of Theological Schools.

In an address to the faculty of the School of Theology in January before accepting the deanship,[6] St. Amant placed his understanding of his new role within the framework of his expectations for Southern Seminary. He hoped

---

[4] According to faculty minutes, the faculty decided to make its first overtures to St. Amant on 13 June 1958, the day after the dismissals, and extended a unanimous invitation on 8 December. After an initial visit in January, St. Amant did not return for serious negotiations until April 1959. On 22 April 1959 President McCall asked the faculty to suggest other names "in light of the fact that Dr. Penrose St. Amant had recently indicated his unreadiness to give an affirmative answer to the invitation that had been extended him." On 4 May McCall announced that St. Amant had accepted the deanship as of 1 June and presented him to the faculty. St. Amant presided over a faculty meeting as Dean of the School of Theology first on 3 June 1959.

[5] A letter of Howard E. Spell to Lamar Jackson, Chairman of the Board, dated 6 May 1959, backed St. Amant's request regarding initiative of the dean in hiring faculty.

[6] The date is 15 January 1958, according to *Minutes*, School of Theology, 14 January 1959, p. 146. St. Amant preserved notes for it on undated note cards and one piece of seminary letterhead dated 1859–1959. A personal diary, however, confirms that the speech was given in January. The notes themselves substantiate that he gave the address before he actually assumed the deanship on 1 June 1959.

the Seminary would be a Christian community (*koinonia*) in which members would not fear disagreement but would disagree as "Christian gentlemen" and be "Christians first." He wanted the Seminary, as an educational institution, to be both a professional and a graduate school. He envisioned the Seminary as both a servant and a leader of the denomination which would "fulfill needs of Southern Baptists and criticize them and lift them to higher levels."

With obvious sensitivity to the need for clarity in a vexed administrative situation he spelled out his understanding of the dean's role pointedly. (1) The dean guides the academic life of the school with alertness both to "trends in theological education" and "nuances of the particular situation." (2) In consultation with appropriate departments he is the focal point in selection of additions to the faculty. (3) He determines the best use of faculty personnel, a matter on which the dean's authority must be clear. (4) He has the same relationship to the faculty of the School of Theology that the president has to the Seminary as a whole. (5) He serves as liaison between students and faculty and between faculty and the president. He "fights for student rights when in jeopardy, defends faculty demands against student lethargy and immaturity." He "fights for faculty rights and welfare when in jeopardy and defends administrative policies against faculty negligence or abuse." (6) He assists faculty members "in finding and realizing personal destinies" through special study, travel, writing, and so forth. (7) As an academician, he strives to be a good teacher, keeping abreast of scholarship in his field, and at the same time develops administrative skills. He must maintain the confidence of colleagues on both faculty and staff.[7]

Addressing himself more directly to the situation, he went on to add that the dean "should move forward from the point of the recent controversy and should not be expected to involve himself in it." He could see no value in rehashing its pros and cons. "[The] best therapy now is work and the forward look." Finally, he explained that he did not "mean to imply that these are conditions on which I will accept the deanship." These would be important factors but not the only ones on which he would accept. Other, more personal ones, would also play a role.

On 12 May shortly after St. Amant accepted the post, the faculty of the School of Theology agreed to

---

[7]The duties of the dean listed by St. Amant resemble to some extent those delineated by the report of the firm of Booz, Allen, and Hamilton, Management Consultants, who studied Southern Seminary during the academic year 1956–57, but they also bear the distinctive St. Amant imprint. The BAH Report, pp. 134–38, noted also that the dean should carry a minimal teaching load, take part in the Seminary's program of research and in denominational leadership and stimulate faculty to do the same, provide prospective students with information about the Seminary, and serve as a member of the deans' council.

recommend to the Board of Trustees that the dean of the School of Theology be given power to designate a director of graduate studies and the professors who would teach in the graduate studies with the understanding that this will be done in consultation with the faculty.[8]

St. Amant stood in a position to act decisively in putting his new house in order.

RESPONDING TO CRISIS

The paramount issue, St. Amant himself perceived, was to eliminate the threat to the Seminary's accreditation.[9] In light of an investigation conducted by an ad hoc committee composed of Deans Oren H. Baker, Gray M. Blandy, and Frank B. Lewis, 24–28 October 1959, the Commission on Accrediting of the American Association of Theological Schools noted "positive steps taken to repair the damage done to the seminary by the events leading up to the dismissal of the thirteen faculty members." But it remained unconvinced "that the seminary has taken adequate steps to repair the damage to the dismissed professors," citing a generally accepted principle in instances of dismissal on grounds other than that of moral turpitude "which would require extension of salaries for a year, whether the dismissed found other employment or not." The Commission also doubted whether "adequate measures have yet been inaugurated to insure the proper exercise of administrative authority in academic matters and to protect the rights of the faculty."

> The Commission did not withdraw accreditation, but it cited the Seminary's unfavorable faculty-student ratio, the inadequacy of its faculty and library for the ambitious program of the School, and especially the shortcomings of its facilities for advanced study leading to the master's and doctor's degrees in theology.

The Commission proceeded to recommend

> a temporary discontinuance of admissions to the Th.M. and Th.D. programs, and specific measures to strengthen the faculty in respect to salaries, opportunities for sabbatical leave and research, and the appointment of scholars trained in other graduate schools of theology, including schools in a university setting.[10]

Even before St. Amant's election, faculty, administration, and trustees had already taken steps to respond to notations and recommendations. His appointment, however, expedited the process still more. In their 19 May 1959 meeting the trustees appointed a committee composed of two faculty mem-

---

[8] Letter of Duke K. McCall to Penrose St. Amant.

[9] Personal interview, Louisville, 20 June 1988.

[10] "Consideration of the report on the Inspection of Southern," Commission on Accrediting, A.A.T.S., 1958–59.

bers (Dale Moody and Wayne E. Oates) and two trustees (O. Norman Shands, Chair of the Trustee Executive Committee, and Lamar Jackson, Chair of the Board of Trustees) with St. Amant as chairperson "to work on the matter of maintaining accreditation." In its initial meeting this committee placed the reins in St. Amant's hands as he had requested. As chairperson, he would serve as the liaison between trustees, administration, faculty, and the A.A.T.S.; handle news releases; inform students; and confer with the A.A.T.S. regarding steps to be taken to retain accreditation.[11]

St. Amant's third "Tentative Report to the Executive Director of the American Association of Theological Schools" reveals how quickly the institution moved, under his leadership, to rectify its problems and put itself back on line.[12] On 12 January 1961, the Executive Committee of the Board of Trustees directed the president of the seminary to pay each professor dismissed the equivalent of a year's salary and benefits "according to his rank and salary as of 12 June 1958." On 6 March the faculty and on 15 March the Board of Trustees adopted a statement on academic freedom and tenure "based on the statement adopted by the American Association of Theological Schools on June 16, 1960."

By the spring of 1962 the Seminary had also acted to remove notations concerning student-faculty ratio, faculty supervising graduate studies, the quality of the graduate program, and the library. Addition of new faculty dropped the student-faculty ratio under 20:1 and solved to some extent the problem of adequate faculty for graduate supervision. Most of the faculty added held advanced degrees from other graduate schools. In response to the notation concerning the Th.D. program the faculty of the School of Theology temporarily suspended admissions to the Th.M. and Th.D. degrees from January 1961 until September 1962 and limited the number of students supervised by a professor to five. Between September 1959 and September 1961 enrollment in graduate studies dropped from 101 to 55. The faculty had already revamped the graduate program, structuring it more definitely and in June of 1959 the dean had appointed a director of graduate studies to coordinate the effort. The program underwent continuous refinement under the direction of Dale Moody (1959–61), Ray Summers (1961–64), Wayne E. Oates (1964–68), and William E. Hull (1968–69).

The report also noted the effects of a strong program for sabbatical leaves which St. Amant administered liberally during this period in order to enhance the quality of the faculty. The program provided for fully funded sabbaticals

---

[11]*Minutes*, School of Theology, 24 June 1959.

[12]The Booz, Allen, and Hamilton Study, completed in January 1957, undoubtedly added impetus, for it had cited some of the same problems. It cited, for instance, the poor faculty-student ratio (35:1), large number of doctoral graduates, and heavy teaching load of faculty as serious problems for quality education. It called for a 15:1 ratio, a scaling back of graduate studies, and employment of new faculty with degrees from other graduate institutions.

every seventh year for all tenured professors as approved by the school dean, president, and trustees. At the same time it made possible early sabbaticals in instances where they would benefit the seminary and its programs. St. Amant strongly encouraged research and publication. In 1967 he announced the possibility of half-sabbaticals.[13]

Library resources, the fourth area evoking a notation, improved markedly. Bound volumes increased from 86,025 in 1958–59 to 121,600 in 1960–61 as a consequence of an increase in expenditures from $21,050 to $37,318. New purchases included several periodicals in foreign languages.

In addition to these efforts to fulfill recommendations of the A.A.T.S., the Board of Trustees also adopted a new salary scale for faculty in March 1960 and a plan, drafted by the dean himself, granting faculty members with children in college $1,000 a year per student up to a maximum of four years amortized over a ten year period. In the 1964–65 academic year in response to pleas from faculty and staff, the trustees elevated the salary scale again.[14]

BEYOND CRISIS

Although Penrose St. Amant directed much of his energy to the threat to Southern Seminary's accreditation, he did not let that become a final resting place. The sixties were turbulent years for the Seminary for reasons other than what happened in 1958. The effort to respond to the crisis generated a level of energy which enabled the School of Theology to respond in remarkably creative ways to some of the other challenges and move to a higher level in the field of training for ministry. In this St. Amant, with a fairly gentle but firm hand, guided the school toward improved training in both professional and graduate programs. In 1961 he warned the faculty about increasingly rapid change, especially in the South, wherein Southern Seminary could stand still only at its peril. Predicting that the seminary would "face pressures from several areas," he urged the faculty to guard against preoccupations neither theological nor practical as the Seminary attempted to be "a denominational Seminary seeking to relate itself in scholarship and life to the Christian world." Southern must avoid the easy way of "glittering generalities" and provide "creative and relevant leadership" or ministry of the future would become "an irrelevant appendage."[15]

St. Amant sought improvement of theological education prior to seminary and in both professional and graduate areas. In a response to a paper by Walter Harrelson, Dean at Vanderbilt Divinity School, 11 June 1964 at a

---

[13]*Minutes*, School of Theology, 6 February.

[14]The question of low salaries also received attention in the Booz, Allen, and Hamilton Study. The report recommended significant increases and ranking with tough procedures for advancement.

[15]Notes on the back of a memo from William E. Hull dated 19 May 1961.

DEAN AT SOUTHERN

symposium sponsored by the A.A.T.S., he criticized excessive stress on graduate rather than professional education and neglect of pre-seminary education. Contrary to widely held sentiment in A.A.T.S. circles, he believed that liberal arts could be effectively taught on a religious track. In the interest of professional education, moreover, he would not hesitate to approve a shift of degree nomenclature (from B.D. to M.Div.) and would encourage a professional S.T.D.

As regards pre-seminary education, St. Amant sought to improve liaison with religion departments of colleges and universities. The latter frequently complained that the seminaries neglected what the colleges offered in preparation for seminary. In addition to commissioning several faculty studies of the problem, St. Amant invited several college professors to serve as visiting professors at Southern between 1965 and 1967. These included Edwin D. Johnston, Mercer University, and Fred D. Howard, Wayland Baptist College, in 1965–66, and Oscar Brooks, William Jewell College, and Edgar V. McKnight, Furman University, in 1966–67.

In the professional area the dean pushed for a professional S.T.D. A faculty committee submitted an initial proposal in October 1963 and a more extended program in January 1964.[16] In the meantime, however, discussion of degree nomenclature in member schools of the A.A.T.S. led toward the professional doctor of ministry degree (D.Min.), thus abbreviating the life of the S.T.D. Only three or four persons actually completed it.

Changes in degree nomenclature do not occur easily, but complaints from professors of religion in colleges, students, and ministers brought continued use of the bachelor of divinity sharply under fire. Southern Seminary proposed use of the master of theology (Th.M) or master of sacred theology (S.T.M.), designations already current,[17] but the A.A.T.S. favored a new designation, the master of divinity (M.Div.). After yielding to the A.A.T.S proposal of the M.Div.,[18] the faculty of the School of Theology worked out an updating program on the basis of A.A.T.S. recommendations which would permit trading of the B.D. for the M.Div.[19] Alumni of Southern prior to 1964 were permitted to trade in the degree by taking eight hours of additional work and writing a research paper. Updating courses were offered in July 1968 and 1969.[20] In an experimental period, in the meantime, other theological schools pressed for a professional doctorate other than the S.T.D, Claremont experimented with a doctor of religion, Chicago a doctor of ministry in 1965. Southern Seminary, however, did not begin a D.Min. program until after St. Amant resigned the deanship.

---

[16]*Minutes*, School of Theology, 6 October 1963; 6 January 1964.

[17]*Minutes*, School of Theology, 2 November 1964; 7 December 1964.

[18]*Minutes*, School of Theology, 1 December 12, 1966; 6 March 1967.

[19]*Minutes*, School of Theology, 1 May 1967.

[20]*Minutes*, School of Theology, 11 September 1987.

As nomenclature underwent revision, St. Amant pushed also for revision of the M.Div. curriculum. In 1965 a Curriculum Committee proposed development of interdisciplinary courses in each of the divisions of the school of theology (Biblical, Historical, Theological, and Practical).[21] Subsequently it recommended development of functional majors.[22] Meanwhile, the School of Theology, responding to prodding by the A.A.T.S., expanded the field education program "designed to integrate classroom teaching with field experience." The new design combined required field work under supervision with "practica" scheduled at the beginning and end of each student's course of study.[23]

The dean also encouraged the development of programs in connection with other local institutions. In January 1966 he and others met with the chairperson of the Department of History at the University of Louisville to consider the offering of a joint degree (M.A./M.Div.) in history. Before his resignation in 1969 the Seminary had obtained accreditation from the Southern Association of Colleges and Schools, become a charter member of Kentuckiana Metroversity, a consortium of eight local schools, and begun to explore the possibility of a Theological Association of Mid-America with four theological schools in the Louisville area.[24]

CONFLICT AND RESIGNATION

Considering the difficulties of the decade, Penrose St. Amant experienced a remarkably smooth tenure as Dean of the School of Theology. Under his leadership the School quickly recovered from the trauma brought on by the firing of thirteen professors and started a slow ascent to a new level of professional and graduate training for Christian ministry. As one would expect, however, progress did not occur without occasional conflict regarding policies and programs, or their implementation. One of these conflicts set the stage for St. Amant's resignation as dean.

On 19 April 1966 the Board of Trustees had approved a sabbatical leave for the 1967–68 academic year for Wayne E. Oates, Professor of Psychology of Religion. Initially Oates presented two possible proposals for the sabbatical: a full year of study in psychology, clinical psychiatry, and other behavioral sciences at the University of North Carolina in Chapel Hill; or a year of study at the William Allison White School of Psychiatry in Washington, D.C. In addition, he was exploring travel to the Orient during the summer of 1968 on behalf of the Foreign Mission Board of the Southern Baptist Convention and in the interest of studying Buddhism and Hinduism as they related to the

---

[21]*Minutes*, School of Theology, 6 December 1965.
[22]*Minutes*, School of Theology, 6 February, 3 April, 1 May 1967.
[23]*Minutes*, School of Theology, 7 February 1966.
[24]*Minutes*, School of Theology, 31 March 1969.

Psychology of Religion.[25] In March 1967 he requested a deferral of his sabbatical from the 1967–68 to the 1968–69 academic year. The Trustees approved this request in their April meeting.[26]

Already during this period, faculty members had begun petitioning for a change in policy which would permit local sabbaticals. In their annual letter to the Trustees adopted 4 March 1968, the faculty of the School of Theology formally requested the Trustees to "consider allowing a Faculty member to stay in Louisville during his [or her] sabbatical, either full or half, in order that he [or she] may write in leisure."[27] In line with this petition, on 7 February 1968 Professor Oates requested a local sabbatical, during which he proposed "to study the problems of the psychopathology of religion" in the Department of Psychiatry of the University of Louisville Medical School, a project already underway. He would not use seminary office facilities so as to limit demands of students on his time. He would, however, continue to supervise six students in a psychiatric information program at Norton during the two semesters. On 25 March Professor Henlee Barnette, who had also deferred his sabbatical one year due to the resignation of a colleague in the Department of Christian Ethics, requested a half-sabbatical to be spent doing research and writing in Louisville.[28] In April St. Amant presented and received approval of both requests in the School of Theology Subcommittee of the Board of Trustees. When they came before the full Board, however, President Duke K. McCall challenged them on the grounds that they violated established policy. The Trustees approved the sabbaticals with the proviso that they be "taken in line with prevailing sabbatical regulations, which does not include local sabbaticals."[29]

The Board of Trustees did not act in the April plenary on the faculty request for a policy revision which would include local sabbaticals. On 12 September 1968, however, the Executive Committee of the Board of Trustees revised the policy on sabbaticals to include a statement reading: "A sabbatical leave to be used in a major research project for which residence in Louisville is required may be granted for a full year at full salary." On 16 September the Deans' Council, conferring with President McCall by phone, unanimously approved the recommendation of Dean St. Amant that the request be approved with assurance that Dr. Oates would not receive additional compensation.[30]

---

[25]Wayne E. Oates, Memo to Penrose St. Amant, 1 April 1966.

[26]*Minutes*, School of Theology Subcommittee, Board of Trustees, 5 April 1967.

[27]School of Theology, Faculty Letter to the Board of Trustees, Adopted 4 March 1968, p. 3.

[28]Henlee H. Barnette, Letter to Penrose St. Amant, 25 March 1968.

[29]*Minutes*, Board of Trustees, April 1968, Items 57 (Oates) and 58 (Barnette).

[30]*Minutes of the Deans' Council*, 16 September 1968.

This disagreement understandably placed a strain on administrative relationships between the dean and the president. From President McCall's point of view, approval of the request required a clearly stated policy. He gave deans freedom to make decisions, but he expected them to keep him informed. He was not fully aware of these proposals until they appeared in the full board meeting, where he blocked them.[31] From Dean St. Amant's point of view the president's objections seemed somewhat "arbitrary." Had McCall made his strong opposition completely clear before the Board met, St. Amant would not have presented the requests of Oates and Barnette to the School of Theology Subcommittee. He would have dealt personally with the disagreement rather than before the full Board.[32]

St. Amant and McCall often stood on opposite sides during the decade of his deanship. His more personal style clashed somewhat with McCall's "adversarial" style. Perhaps because of close personal friendship not broken by disagreement, he laid aside thoughts of resigning at times before this. For two or three years he had contemplated retirement to return to teaching. "Ten years are enough," he thought. He wanted to spend the remaining years of his career teaching church history at Southern Seminary.[33]

A REFLECTION

St. Amant disclosed in this decision the good sense of timing which characterized his administration. He never acted precipitously, but, once he had sized up a situation, he made up his mind and acted decisively. Decisiveness proved crucial in responding to the complex and intricate set of problems he met when he came in 1959. It helped to push aside the community's tendency to bog down in the past, especially in analysis of what went wrong, and directed its energies into positive channels. Much credit must go to this trait for the Seminary's rapid recovery.

St. Amant manifested throughout his administration a remarkable feeling for the right balance of concerns: the denomination and the world of theological education, professional and graduate education, faculty and administration, students and faculty, church and society. In comments to the faculty he frequently apprised them of the undercurrents in both denominational life and academia and encouraged genuine scholarship addressed to the churches. While seeking to rectify the deficiencies of the graduate program noted by the A.A.T.S., he spurred enhancement of professional training in ways that helped to put Southern Seminary on the cutting edge of American theological education. Although partial by vocation to faculty and students, he maintained good rapport with administrative colleagues. As a church historian special-

---

[31]Phone interview, 15 August 1988.
[32]Personal interview, Louisville, 20 June 1988.
[33]Personal interview, Louisville, 20 June 1988.

izing in the field of American religion, he possessed unusual gifts for interpreting the interplay of church and society, and he himself modeled a deep appreciation for culture in service of Christian ministry that impacted the thinking of both colleagues and students.

St. Amant's most significant contribution, however, probably lay in the consistent confidence he instilled in colleagues. Possessed of a naturally self-effacing personality, he quietly drew out "gifts" of the faculty with suggestions, assignments, or requests. In an interview he confessed that he lives with a kind of "cosmic sorrow" which raises his level of concern for the less gifted. In his role as dean, I can attest on the basis of personal experience, he had a way of undergirding individual faculty members in times of illness, stress, or distress. When I experienced severe voice problems that threatened my career while still an instructor, St. Amant did not "pass by" me "on the other side." Not only did he keep in touch with my situation, he arranged a vacation and put me in touch with the right sources of help. Although my difficulties persisted right up to the time for my appointment as an assistant professor, he risked a one-year contract, then a three-year one. As my problem relented rapidly during that time, he speeded-up the process so that I received tenure, a promotion, and a sabbatical after four years as assistant professor. He did similar things for other colleagues.

As much as St. Amant excelled in personal aspects of administration, he fared only moderately well in organizational and communicational aspects. Teaching at the graduate level at the same time, he delegated much responsibility to others. He failed to keep careful records, for instance, of his own addresses and of administrative exchanges with faculty or staff. Consequently, communication sometimes got snarled and required extra attention. Inadequate attention to detail may explain in part the painful confusion and conflict over sabbatical policies. Yet St. Amant's overall success as dean shows that, if administrators are to err, as all do, it is better to err on the organizational than on the personal side. Even in this difficult situation, St. Amant never let disagreement and frustration cloud his personal friendship with McCall; in his own mind he distinguished administrative and personal relationships. As a result, he could retire from the deanship without rancor and resume the role of a professor or, as it turned out, assume the presidency of The Baptist Theological Seminary in Rüschlikon, Switzerland, during a sabbatical leave there. Both behind and ahead, all roads lay open to him.

C. PENROSE ST. AMANT: PRESIDENT AT RÜSCHLIKON

G. KEITH PARKER
Baptist Theological Seminary
8803 Rüschlikon, Switzerland

When a film about the International Baptist Theological Seminary in Rüschlikon, Switzerland, was made, a creative, yet descriptive, title was chosen: "Rüschlikon: Bridge to the Future." In many ways the term could also be used for Penrose St. Amant because he was a "bridging" president, one whose gifts and unique leadership actually bridged the past, present and future, as well as the multiple cultures and tasks the Seminary faced. Elected to the post in 1971 and arriving on the campus the following year, St. Amant was no stranger to either the European scene or the unusual ministry and complexities of Rüschlikon.[1]

An eminent and respected scholar, historian and teacher, Penrose St. Amant came with European experience, having completed a doctorate in Scotland in the early 1950s, having traveled extensively in Europe, North Africa and the Middle East, and having had one sabbatical in Paris and another in Rüschlikon. While there in 1970–71 he re-wrote his entire survey of church history and has used it as a syllabus ever since; that syllabus has also become a popular tool for students across Europe, especially many from Eastern Europe who have attended his lectures in the SITE (Summer Institute for Theological Education) Program. He has continued after retirement to assist in SITE teaching, both on campus and as a traveling lecturer in East-bloc countries.

In August 1964, long before his own consideration as president, St. Amant gave the main lecture entitled "Of What Use is History?" at the Opening Convocation when John D. W. Watts was inaugurated as president. A clear bridging challenge is laid before the school, with a call for balance and especially for a broader basis for mission and practical concerns. In many ways the statement anticipates the balance he eventually brought to the presidency there.

> Until recently, history has been a secondary concern of Baptists. We are a practical people. Especially in America our genius has been in promotion, evangelism, and missions. Theological and historical interests have not been paramount. We tend to start in the New Testament and then "leap over"

---

[1] Hereafter the word "Rüschlikon" is used as an abbreviation for the International Baptist Theological Seminary and Baptist Center located in the Swiss village of that name, a popular practice among Baptists world-wide, but not strictly accurate and not always understood within Switzerland.

the history of Christianity and land with both feet firmly planted in the seventeenth century, with a backward glance at Luther and Calvin. This is probably the result primarily of a sectarian and separatist strain in our heritage. It has strengthened our sense of mission but also has tended at times to remove us from the mainstream of Protestant life and thought. A deeper sense of history paradoxically will sharpen our Baptist sense of mission and also relate us more significantly to the major thrusts of Protestantism. Concerning Baptists it is not far wrong to say that we have been so busy making history we have forgotten to record it and have neglected its lessons.[2]

When Penrose and Jessie St. Amant were appointed as missionaries by the Foreign Mission Board and approved by the Trustees of the Seminary at Rüschlikon there was a sense in which a bridge was being re-built in terms of strengthening that sense of mission and theological/historical reflection. What St. Amant brought to the Seminary and was able to do can be best understood in the historical context of the school. Because of the long, *complicated* history preceeding the actual foundation of the school, some details are given to set the stage, then a brief portrayal of the Swiss setting is made, followed by a sketch of the St. Amant presidency.

RÜSCHLIKON: A LONG DREAM

In the October 1988 meeting of the Foreign Mission Board a most significant decision was made:

> that the Foreign Mission Board transfer ownership of the seminary property in Rüschlikon, Switzerland to the European Baptist Federation, to fulfill our goal of indigenization and in response to the expressed desire of the European Baptist Federation to accept responsibility for the seminary.[3]

Two other historical events preceeded this event by 80 and by 40 years: the original idea and plea in 1908 for an international Baptist college or university in Europe and the actual purchase of the property in Zürich in 1948.

The dream of a world wide cooperation and fellowship of Baptists came into being in London in 1905 with the first congress and establishment of the Baptist World Alliance.[4] The same spirit led to European conferences in Ber-

---

[2]Penrose St. Amant, "Of What Use is History?" *Baptist Theological Seminary Bulletin* (Rüschlikon: Schuck, 1964–65) 4.

[3]*Minutes* of the Foreign Mission Board, 10–12 October 1988, 15.

[4]J. D. Hughey, *Baptist Partnership in Europe* (Nashville: Broadman Press, 1982) 113.

lin in 1908 and in Stockholm in 1913.[5] In the former meeting a resolution was passed unanimously urging the establishment of "an international European Baptist college (Hochschule) in a central place."[6] The appeal for strengthening the very few existing continental seminaries was also made but the focus was clear that "especially gifted young men" could have opportunity to study elsewhere in an international Baptist context.[7] Professor Benander, director of the Swedish Baptist Seminary, spoke to the congress, calling for a "great European Baptist University."[8]

Between the European Congress of 1908 and the Baptist World Alliance Congress of 1911 much research was done to locate a place appropriate for the school. Baptist World Alliance (hereafter, BWA) minutes show that they considered Constantinople, Budapest, Berlin, and even a site in Bulgaria.[9] The Baptist Union of Great Britian and Ireland, who had done most of the study, proposed that the school be located in Berlin and have trustees from the Southern Baptist Convention, the Northern Baptist Convention and from Canada. The property would be owned by the BWA. The projected site was changed to St. Petersburg at the BWA Congress in Philadelphia due to the strong presence and appeals from the Russian delegation. The story of their persecution and urgent need for education for ministry led to very dramatic appeal for "a great cosmopolitan Theological seminary in the heart of Europe."[10] Although there were brief attempts to consider other sites such as Rome and Moscow, the impetus remained with St. Petersburg and money was raised, reaching $100,000 by 1948. Although property was bought and some attempts were made in Russia, the ensuing political changes essentially put a stop to the impetus.

Although Southern Baptists were very active in the BWA proceedings and especially in raising money for the projects, apparently very early some had thought of Zürich as a possibility for a Baptist school due to its central location and Anabaptist heritage. W. O. Carver, professor of missions at Southern Baptist Seminary in Louisville, wrote to George W. Sadler in 1948 that he and Everett Gill, Foreign Mission Board representative in Europe, had

---

[5]F. W. Simoleit, ed., *Offizieller Bericht über den 1. Kongress der europäischen Baptisten* (Kassel: Buchdruckerei des Verlagshaus der deutschen Baptisten, 1908) 330. Cited by Carol Woodfin, "Rueschlikon: The Establishment and Early Development of an International Baptist Theological Seminary in the Heart of Post-War Europe" (M.A. thesis, Wake Forest University, 1987) 3. The Woodfin study represents the only complete study of the Rüschlikon story. She is uniquely qualified, not only by historical methodology, but also by her own years of experience there, first when her father was professor, then later as a student, and then while working for the European Baptist Press Service there.

[6]Woodfin, "Rueschlikon," 3.
[7]Ibid., 4.
[8]Ibid.
[9]Ibid., 4, 5.
[10]Baptist World Alliance *Minutes*, 1911, 240–41. Cited by Woodfin, "Rueschlikon," 6.

discussed the possibility forty years previously.¹¹ Gill, who lived in Rome, and Carver met in Switzerland on occasion for family vacations.

In 1920 Baptists met in London to coordinate relief efforts on the continent; the conference dealt also with urgent educational needs in Europe. Travel commissions gave reports from the BWA and the Southern Baptist Convention. One speaker noted that the following seminaries were needed: one in Prague (for Slavs), one in Bucharest (for Romanians), one in Helsinki (for Finns but also with work for Lettish and Lithuanian) and a *central one for the Latin countries*.¹² Noting that the Roman Catholics had international education in Rome, the Southern Baptists apparently wanted the central school there. The London conference report indicated that the students would come from Romania, Italy, France, Switzerland, Belgium, Spain, Portugal and perhaps from Brazil and other countries in South America.¹³

The London conference formed a Committee on Education which set out resolutions that were adopted by the Conference and set the guiding direction that would later result in the selection of Rüschlikon. The call was for each country to set preparatory work and to send some students for further training to the U. S. and England. Baptist seminaries in Europe "should be established, where possible, in the neighborhood of universities."¹⁴ At the same conference an allocation system was set out to avoid duplication: Southern Baptists would work in Spain, Yugoslavia, Hungary, Italy, Romania, the Ukraine and other parts of Russia. The countries were to be served mostly after Rüschlikon was founded.¹⁵

J. H. Rushbrook of London was appointed as Commissioner for Europe to work with the different groups, and Everett Gill became the Foreign Mission Board (hereafter, FMB) "Representative in Europe," serving from 1921 to 1939 and living in Lausanne, Switzerland but traveling widely throughout Europe; he played a key role in helping establish several national seminaries in this period. At the BWA Stockholm meeting of 1923 the call was once again made for a Baptist University, "where the best men and women of our Church shall teach. . . . (They) shall come together from all countries for one or two years, where their eyes may be opened for the wonders of the Kingdom of God. They go back into their old surroundings and let the light which they have received here shine out there."¹⁶

---

¹¹Hughey, *Baptist Partnership*, 116.

¹²Woodfin, "Rueschlikon," 11.

¹³"Report of London Conference," *Baptist Times and Freeman* (London) 30 July 1920, 504. Cited by Woodfin, 12.

¹⁴Ibid.

¹⁵Woodfin, "Rueschlikon," 13.

¹⁶Baptist World Alliance *Minutes*, Stockholm, 1923, 140. Cited by Woodfin, "Rueschlikon," 14, 15.

After World War II Southern Baptists undertook ambitious efforts in many areas including education. Taking the initiative for an international seminary in Switzerland was part of those efforts but also included much of the thought and study of the previous years. Dr. George W. Sadler was successor to Gill, and now called FMB Area Secretary for Europe, Africa and the Near East. The massive post war effort of the FMB was called "Advance" and led by Dr. Theron Rankin who became Executive Secretary of the FMB in 1945. Sadler's travels and reports on war-torn Europe included the idea and proposal for the school. He had consulted with others such as John Allen Moore, FMB refugee worker in Egypt and former teacher in Yugoslavia and Hungary, and the BWA Executive Secretary. J. D. Franks, FMB relief worker in Geneva, proposed to Dr. Sadler that they set up "a really *great* seminary, one equal to the best to be found in any land, designed to serve not only a few national Baptist groups in central and southeastern Europe, but all European Baptist constituencies."[17] Southern Baptist state papers and FMB publicity posters between 1947 and 1948 solicited support for the project of "A European Baptist Seminary for Post-Graduate Students."[18]

In 1947 the BWA Congress met in Copenhagen and many contacts were re-established among European Baptists. Rankin, Sadler and Franks attended and theological education was the topic of several sessions. The destruction of the war had interrupted most education and there was a scarcity of preachers. A post-war conference was to be set up similiar to the one in 1920; Rankin and Sadler were on the planning committee.

In April 1948, the FMB met to discuss the "Advance" program and theological education for national leaders was part of the mission strategy set out by Rankin.[19] Sadler's report on Europe included a need for a "full-fledged first class theological seminary."[20] The FMB set aside money to establish an international seminary in Geneva, a first for the FMB. In August 1948 the BWA sponsored conference met in London to deal with cooperative work among Baptists in rebuilding after the war. Sadler announced the FMB decision which was met "with anything but enthusiasm."[21]

Apparently offense was taken to an article written by Franks in *The Commission*, the FMB magazine, depicting rather graphically the conditions in Europe; his appeal was to an American readership to raise funds but depicted Baptists in Europe as weak and as needing help from the U. S. He also sug-

---

[17]J. D. Franks, mimeographed notes, Rüschlikon, 1–3. Cited by Woodfin, "Rueschlikon," 10.

[18]Woodfin, "Rueschlikon," 21.

[19]Ibid., 25.

[20]George W. Sadler, "Report to the Board," Foreign Mission Board *Minutes*, 6 April 1948, 16. Cited by Woodfin, 25.

[21]George W. Sadler, "Historical Sketch," mimeographed notes, Rüschlikon, 1. Cited by Woodfin, "Rueschlikon," 27.

gested that the school should serve all of Europe, but there had been no consultation on this part of the proposal. Most felt such a program should be under the BWA or at least under European direction. The motives of the Americans were questioned. J. D. Hughey also attended the conference and often said that the objection was not so much to the idea of the school or its obvious need but rather to the *way* it was done, as a *fait accompli*.

The conference did thank the Southern Baptists for their generosity; they also abandoned the old allocation system.[22] The seminary would now be free to be totally international in Europe.

Forty years later, in October, 1988, the Foreign Mission Board was faced with the willingness of the European Baptist Federation to accept full ownership; the FMB voted to turn it over completely, bringing to a completion some of the original thinking and hopes. In the 1978 financial crisis related to the dollar collapse, FMB Area Secretary J. D. Hughey had made the same offer, but only administrative responsibilities were accepted at that time. St. Amant's presidency had prepared the Europeans in some ways for the administrative responsibilities, mostly through the increased engagement of trustees into Rüschlikon life. His own expressed desire was always to make it fully European and yet to keep a level of partnership with the FMB. That eventually was the solution given.

RÜSCHLIKON: THE SETTING

On 8 October 1948, the Foreign Mission Board finalized the purchase of the Leo Bodmer estate overlooking the Lake of Zürich in the small village of Rüschlikon, located in the Canton of Zürich. The villa had about forty rooms and was built in 1927; the property totaled about eight acres and had a gardner's house. The purchase price was one million Swiss francs, just over a quarter million dollars at that time.

In addition to the presence of Bodmer at the Thalwil land office signing, there were also the Watts, Franks and Moores, representing the FMB, W. O. Lewis, representing the Northern Baptists, and several Swiss Baptist pastors.[23]

Many factors were involved in the decision of this location, not the least of which was the availability of such an unusual piece of property. But it was clear also that the strength of the German-speaking Baptists, the neutrality of Switzerland during and after two world wars, and the stability of Swiss society played roles. Also, the fact that the Anabaptists had their beginnings in Zürich and the early missionary work in Zürich of Johann Gerhard Oncken, sometimes called the "Father" of European Baptists, contributed to the selection of Zürich.

---

[22]Woodfin, ibid., 28–29.
[23]Ibid., 34.

Of these factors, the most vital one in the post-war years was Swiss *neutrality* which meant that in Rüschlikon men and women could meet from both East and West Europe. Not only during the "Cold War" period was this vital but also during the St. Amant years, for Rüschlikon quickly became the main home for conferences, meetings of leaders, and consultations not only because of its facilities, but also very much due to the neutral Swiss location.

The sense of openness and cooperation was underlined in the opening of the School which included representatives of the Southern Baptist Convention, the Northern Baptists, The Baptist World Alliance, the World Council of Churches, the Swiss Free Churches, the Swiss Reformed Church, and many others. Emil Brunner represented the University of Zürich, and the BWA General Secretary gave the main address.[24]

Part of the uniqueness of the history and setting was the decision by the FMB not to have the school and operation set up as a "mission" as one finds in other FMB settings. This perhaps developed, but nevertheless the original plan was unique since the mission organization has been the main administrative tool in all other places of service. A practical result of this arrangement was that the American and European professors were to be on an equal footing as far as possible. Salaries were set the same and the same high academic requirements were required.

Trustees were appointed in 1949, meeting first in 1950, "to act as liason between the seminary and their own national Baptist constituency, and to assist in selecting and recommending the right kind of students."[25] In addition to carrying on the other traditions of academic excellence, cooperation and equality, Penrose St. Amant was perhaps strongest in his strengthening the appropriate use of the Trustees. He saw the unique opportunities of their coming together and organized them into committees, with specific assignments and suggestions for the betterment of the school and its programs. Several changes and developments came from these meetings over the years, including changes in the curriculum, strengthening practical theology, and establishing places for students to serve in summer church experiences. In addition, the meetings of Trustees became occasions for the key leaders of European Baptist to meet on other matters, for meetings of the Federation and of committees and special consultations were always held at the trustee meeting time.

It was thus natural that many European Baptist organizations for service started at Rüschlikon. The European Baptist Federation itself grew out of the same 1948 London Conference that announced the foundation of Rüschlikon and was finally planned and put together in Rüschlikon, 8 October 1949.[26]

---

[24]Ibid., 54, 55.
[25]*Trustee Minutes*. Cited by Woodfin, ibid., 69.
[26]Woodfin, ibid., 101.

Other work in missions, evangelism, women's work, and so forth, began at the same setting, especially during the 1950 post-war years when the Cold War made East-West cooperation difficult. During those very tense years, the meetings at Rüschlikon often birthed ideas and concrete plans for pulling the broader Baptist family in Europe together. In discussing an appeal to the FMB not to lose the property, one European leader said in 1988, "It is our home, our birthplace as European Baptists."[27]

The St. Amant years strengthened this broader European perspective, encouraging conferences, meetings and dialogue, not only within Baptist ranks but also with other church groups active in Europe and even with some government officials from Eastern Bloc countries in appeals to let students study at Rüschlikon. There were times when we had to be "checked out" by visits of investigators from those countries, and the gentle spirit, open dialogue, and diplomatic skill of St. Amant played a key role in the later admission of students from those countries. Also notable was the celebration of the 450th anniversary of Anabaptist beginnings in Zürich, carried out by the Seminary, the BWA and the Mennonite Central Committee, drawing world scholars and churchmen. St, Amant also maintained the strong historical working relationship with the University of Zürich. Over the years many Baptists were able to obtain a doctorate there, due to a cooperation with Rüschlikon, and credit given for Seminary work. In the early post-war days, this was a rare opportunity for a free churchman on the continent.

RÜSCHLIKON: THE PRESIDENCY

Penrose St. Amant became the fourth president, following Josef Nordenhaug (1950–60), J. D. Hughey (1960–64) and John Watts, (1964–70). When the seminary was first organized, J. D. Franks functioned as chief administrator; George Sadler, FMB Europe Secretary, was called to be Acting President until a permanent president could be found. Between the Watts' presidency and that of St. Amant, John Allen Moore served one year as interim, and three faculty members (Meister, Wagner and Moorefield) served as rotating chairmen of the faculty until St. Amant could complete his sabbatical commitment to Southern Seminary. He was elected in the summer of 1971 and began his work on campus a year later.

St. Amant was aware of the intensive efforts of his predecessors and made frequent reference to their uniqueness and their contributions. Remarks from his inaugural address are an example:

> As I stand here today, I am keenly aware of those who have shaped the life of this Seminary. Let me recall the large vision of George W. Sadler; the creative imagination of J. D. Franks; the brilliant leadership of that stalwart

---

[27]Knud Wumpelmann, statement at the European Baptist Federation Council, Dorfweil, Germany, 30 September 1988.

Scandanavian Josef Nordenhaug; the perceptive guidance of J. D. Hughey . . . ; the deep devotion of John D. W. Watts, who served more than two decades here as professor, dean, and president; the versatile service of John Allen Moore. . . .[28]

He also expressed eloquently, and with clear perception, deep insight into the role of the Seminary and the presidency. His own words as he looked as the prospect of the future reflect much of the content and direction that his years of service would bring:

> No man who, for almost three decades, has been associated with theological education as teacher and dean in two Southern Baptist seminaries in America could come to the presidency here without some realization of its significant past and its extraordinary prospects; without some awe of its responsibilities and some humbleness before its opportunities; without a sense of obligation to all he can to maintain for it its proper place among the theological schools of the world.[29]

One cannot understand Penrose St. Amant's presidency apart from his practice of the presidency: a devoutly dedicated *search for a theological community of learning*. He was a firm but caring leader, a person sensitive to the complexities of his task and unwilling to yield to the easiest, most pragmatic or administratively economical way out of situations. He was decisive when the time came, but was supremely sensitive to the fact that he was always dealing with human beings. In a discussion of theological community he warned of the peril of sentimentality that might substitute feelings for action, especially under the deep influence of historical Pietism.[30] Always seeking a balance or healthy tension between inevitable opposites, St. Amant also supported the creative, charismatic element in Christianity, underlining the need for *koinonia*.

> My point is not to play down the charismatic side but to say that tender feelings about each other must be something more than a psychological glow induced by prayer and exhortation. Such feelings must be rooted in a common participation in the "new creation "in Christ (II Cor 5:17). Genuine *koinonia* means a common participation in the same spirit and the translation of kindly feelings into concrete action within and beyond the Christian community. . . . Good intentions are not enough. Deeds are required. Otherwise our feelings accomplish little and may actually militate against the community we feel deeply about.[31]

---

[28]Penrose St. Amant, "The Christian Ministry in the 1970's," Inaugaural Address Manuscript, 26 September 1972, 1.

[29]Ibid.

[30]Penrose St. Amant, "The Possibilities and Perils of a Theological Community," Convocation Address Manuscript, 5 January 1971, 1, 2.

[31]Ibid., 2, 3.

St. Amant, in his presidential search for community, warned of talk separated from action, especially because "we who form the theological community are vulnerable . . . because we are experts with words, technicians with talk, professionals where our various vocabularies are concerned."[32] Closer to the core of his search for a theological community is the ongoing creative tension between differing elements; functionally seen, his presidency was to bridge the many elements in a positive way.

> [The theological community] is both a Christian and an academic community and yet it is neither a church nor a university in a full fledged sense, though it is marked by elements of both. Because a Seminary is a Christian community, it seeks to bring into play Divine resources of wisdom, power, and forgiveness, unavailable to a purely academic institution. Because a Seminary is also an academic community its members function on various levels of status an[d] significance.[33]

Rüschlikon was not immune to the general turmoil in Europe in the late 1960s and early 1970s, especially amongst students from central European universities. St. Amant categorized students into three groups: (a) a small minority of radical activists who make headlines; (b) complacent, content students who complain only about restrictions in their own lives; and (c) thoughtful students "who are appalled by the violent tactics of the militants yet sympathize somewhat with their indignation and are attracted by their ardor."[34] The last was the largest group and demanded his deepest interest because they were, above all, willing to participate in dialogue.[35] His expressed goal was to relate dialogically to students and he was a master at just that, not only to students but also faculty and staff alike. He did not favor one group: he was also able to challenge the complacency of many and definitely gave leadership or direction to the dissatisfied few. At the core of the St. Amant presidency was always genuine dialogue, a dynamic community with candor and openness.

As president, St. Amant was also an educator and churchman, calling again and again for keeping perspective. His enthusiasm for learning was contagious.

> All of us, teachers and students alike, need to stretch our minds to grapple with the explosion of knowledge in our time. Let us uphold the ideals of freedom of research, criticism, and dissent—ideals never really popular with some businessmen, legislators, and ecclesiastical leaders, though paraded annually in graduation oratory. Let us follow truth as blind men long for light, insisting upon evidence for our judgements in life as well as library

---

[32]Ibid., 3.
[33]Ibid., 5.
[34]Ibid., 6.
[35]Ibid.

and laboratory. It is amazing how many educated people will require evidence for just about everything except rumor. Let us seek to be good citizens with proper concern for the political process and for civilized values—in short, humanists in the best sense. I speak of Christian humanism, of course.[36]

Balance and perspective were often posited in terms of dangers:

> Twin perils of the theological community are scholarship detached from vocational considerations, and vocational considerations detached from scholarship. The first peril is scholarship detached from the church. The second peril is the pursuit of practical ends devoid of the necessary criticism which scholarly perspective provides. A theological school detached from the church is as unthinkable to me as a medical school detached from medical practice.[37]

Likewise, St. Amant firmly declared that the structure of the Christian faith must be tied to concrete experience and life; he saw this as a gap that needed bridging in the theological community.

> A continual interplay between them should be sought not only in our witness to the world but also in the theological community itself. If the Christian gospel is really good news, it means a celebration of life, despite its cynicism, sorrow and tragedy.[38]

St. Amant's presidency was always in touch with the realities of human nature, but was nevertheless overarched by the Divine dimension. Warning of "false ultimates," he was aware that original sin was not abstract nor was it far from a theological community.[39] Acknowledging the rich heritage of Rüschlikon and the inspiration of former leaders, he also warned about the universal temptation of all leaders "to identify our little plans with the Divine purpose and to equate partial perspectives, personal ambitions and parochial views with ultimate concerns."[40]

If any one point focused upon his presidency beyond his own personal warmth, his humility and academic excellence, it would be his deep *faith, lived and expressed*. His ideal theological community in the final analysis was to be centered on the cross of Christ. Warning of the dangers of treating the cross mainly as a matter of intellectual curiosity, he stressed our *participation* in it. His own words come close to describing the focus of his presidency:

> What does the cross mean? Christ put into mighty deed God's eternal attitude toward man. He could not care more! God cares and the world will

---

[36]Ibid., 8.
[37]Ibid., 8, 9.
[38]Ibid., 9.
[39]Ibid., 11.
[40]Ibid.

glimpse it only when it sees those who say they love him really caring for each other, when it sees something of the sacrificial love of the cross in our lives. I speak not of sentimentality but of unselfish concern. The cross is not only the supreme agency of Divine redemption but is also the supreme symbol of self-sacrifice, openness and forgiveness. Sometimes this means the heroic deeds of a Dietrich Bonhoeffer. More often it means a cheery word, a funny story, interest in another. It means feelings of concern translated into deeds. It means that our words of hope and our sense of victory become flesh for each other and for the world. It means that the cross is less a pretty ornament at the end of a necklace or a neat theological doctrine and more, much more, the central element on the Christian life.[41]

A PERSONAL POSTSCRIPT

When one looks at a powerful personality who influences others and one's own person, one can make generalities and fairly clear points. When, however, the quiet, deep running stream of the life and faith of a true gentle giant like Penrose St. Amant affects you, it is much harder to be precise or descriptive. My own pilgrimage to seminary was circuitous; my first exposure to him was uneventful and yet fascinating in that he was interested not only in church history but also in me as a person.

Later as I was asked to be Garrett Teaching Fellow in history and then worked with him in guiding my doctoral dissertation, I worked much closer and began to appreciate the depth and very personal way of approaching teaching that he had. Later as I was appointed by the FMB to teach at Rüschlikon (1969) I had no idea that he might also come to Rüschlikon as President. When he and Jessie, along with the aging poodle Pierre, did join us in Switzerland, it was a pleasure to work with him in a totally different culture and challenge. I also served as conference director, working with him in additional administration along with the many faculty duties.

Over the years since, however, I have come to appreciate more of his influence on my own life and pilgrimage in Europe. I cannot quote lines of widsom or advice—such would be unlike him—but I am aware that his search for balance and perspective, his approach to teaching and—later in FMB matters—to administration have profoundly affected me. In some ways, my wife, Jonlyn, and I have participated in about two decades of Baptist life and history in Europe; we can say that in many ways St. Amant was a stable and most positive influence on both persons and events. The impact was probably more in terms of building bridges of trust and laying more of a stabilizing foundation for greater European cooperation. We feel fortunate that we were present for some of that; we are also thankful that the St. Amants walked part of the way with us.

---

[41]Ibid., 12, 13.

C. PENROSE ST. AMANT: PREACHER OF THE GOSPEL

W. MORGAN PATTERSON
Georgetown College, Georgetown KY 40324

Penrose St. Amant is a teacher, an administrator, an author and a distinguished lecturer on subjects of theology, church history, the Baptist heritage, religion and culture, and educational issues. But he is also a superb preacher! Although his life and ministry have been given to the classroom and educational administration, he is as much at home in the pulpit as he is behind the teacher's lectern.

Indeed, his ministry has included a calling to preach, and he has regularly served the churches in this role. Over a period of fifty years, he has effectively filled the pulpit on Sundays, served as interim pastor, taught Bible studies, and preached in a variety of special services in the United States and in Europe.

During the 1950s when St. Amant was professor at the New Orleans Baptist Seminary, he was the regular preacher on the seminary's weekly radio program, "Faith for Life," and many of his sermons were printed. They dealt with themes touching doctrine, evangelism, the Christian life and commitment, and Baptist practice. They were carefully focused, strongly biblical, pungently clear, and personally relevant to the needs of people. Furthermore, they were simple and direct, designed to offer spiritual challenge, correction, and comfort.

Earlier, in 1949, one of his sermons was selected to appear in the volume of *Best Sermons* edited by G. Paul Butler. St. Amant's topic was "Christian Faith Confronts the Modern Mind," and his text was taken from 2 Corinthians 4:8: "We are troubled on every side, yet not distressed; we are perplexed but not in despair."

In this sermon, he describes and laments the pervasive influence of secularism in modern society. In turn, he points to the impact which secularism has had on three areas of modern life: art, music, and literature. The situation is one where God is ignored and the Christian faith is viewed as unimportant and irrelevant.

Even with his high view of the value and need of education, St. Amant is nonetheless critical of the position which implies that spiritual problems can be addressed and corrected merely by more and better education. His contention is summarized, in effect, by the statement that "the failure of modern culture to do justice to the Christian doctrine of sin is one of the most disastrous errors of our time."[1]

---

[1] G. Paul Butler, ed., *Best Sermons 1949–1950 Edition* (New York: Harper & Brothers Publishers, 1949) 128.

St. Amant holds that in large measure the ills of modern life are directly traceable to the fact that the Christian doctrines of sin and grace are not understood and that the values of the Christian faith have been abandoned. After identifying the nature and the source of the "modern spirit," he affirms his own faith and declares the good news of the New Testament, namely, that there is mercy and meaning in Christ.

The sermon offers a penetrating look at some of the misguided aspects of modern culture and the failure of moderns to diagnose adequately our troubled spiritual condition. At the same time, he is quick to point to those special insights of the gospel which speak directly to the plight of humanity and provide the very answers contemporary humans seek.

In March 1949, St. Amant spoke to the New Orleans Ministerial Union on the subject of "Prophetic Preaching in a Secular World." His remarks were warmly received, and the president of the Union, Harvey T. Whaley, wrote in a letter to Dr. Roland Q. Leavell that "the time, the circumstances, and probably our own needs most of all, produced an unusual response to Dr. St. Amant's presentation."[2] In fact, Canon William S. Turner, rector of Trinity Episcopal Church, proposed that the sermon be printed in order for it to be available to the members of the Union for further study.

In his perceptive examination of preaching and its challenges, St. Amant dealt with the content of preaching, the dangers faced by preachers, the mood of the congregation to whom preaching is directed, and the resources of the gospel to provide solutions. The theme focuses on the response which Christian preaching can make to the influence of secularism in contemporary society.

In his address, St. Amant first gives consideration to the nature of the gospel. After suggesting what the gospel is *not*, he invokes the words of the Apostle Paul to epitomize the gospel: "God was in Christ reconciling the world unto himself."[3] The heart of the gospel is found in "the Incarnation of God in Jesus Christ and in the Atonement. . . . 'God was in Christ'—this is the Incarnation; 'reconciling the world unto himself'—this is the Atonement."[4]

Those dangers faced by preachers in the task of proclamation include the subtle tendency to use the Word of God to sanctify human words, a superficial quest for application, and the failure to relate the gospel to our day, which results in a "magnificent irrelevance."

As for those to whom preaching is directed, he charges that the mind of modern man is characterized by a secular outlook. But man's plight is "not

---

[2]Letter from Harvey T. Whaley to Roland Q. Leavell, 10 March 1949. (Dr. Whaley was minister of the St. Charles Avenue Baptist Church in New Orleans, and Dr. Leavell was president of the New Orleans Baptist Theological Seminary.)

[3]2 Cor 5:19.

[4]Manuscript, "Prophetic Preaching in a Secular World."

so much the product of an ignorance which enlightenment can allay," it is "a conflict between God and man produced by sin."[5] The Christian faith offers not only an understanding of man's condition but a solution, and it is this: "The grace of God through Jesus Christ is the only power which is able to grapple adequately with the power of sin."

As preacher, St. Amant consistently stresses the reality of sin and the need of redemption. His exposure of the secular characteristics of modern thinking is incisive, and he calls for a prophetic audacity to respond to them. Thus, it is the task of the pulpit to discern and counter the rationalizations created by man's ingenuity and to declare a gospel which emphasizes God's grace as manifested in Jesus Christ. On another occasion, reflecting on the essence of preaching, he noted that it can be summed up by declaring a gospel which has at its center the person of Christ "who is the revelation of God and redeemer of man." This is where preaching must begin.[6]

In a published sermon of a different type, St. Amant based his remarks on the touching story of a Little League baseball team from Monterrey, Mexico. It is entitled "How Tall Is a Giant?" Because the boys on the team were small, it was a wonder that they were able to reach the World Series tournament at Williamsport, Pennsylvania. They were not given much chance to win, but their spirit and determination propelled them finally to victory and to the world championship.

St. Amant then asked, "How tall is a giant?" As tall as courage! As tall as faith! As tall as a dream! He added,

> a giant is taller than despair, taller than doubt, taller than depression. He is taller than his adversaries, taller than circumstances which threaten him, taller than hate and envy and strife, taller than all of his unanswered questions, taller than all his tears.[7]

These are also the qualities needed for our times. The text for the sermon is Hebrews 11:8–10, 13–16, which highlights the pilgrimage of Abraham, in whose life the elements of courage, faith, and a dream are to be found.

In this brief homily are to be found poetry, illustrative material, structure, and biblical insight. It is a model of simplicity, inspiration, and a story well told.

In his preaching St. Amant has frequently grappled with some of the most puzzling aspects of life—the anomalies, the paradoxes, the contradictions—which perplex the mind but sometimes result in heightened faith. His sermon, "Strength from Weakness," is an example, and his text is 2 Corinthians 12:7–10.

---

[5]Ibid.

[6]Manuscript, "Christian Preaching and Modern Man."

[7]W. Morgan Patterson and Raymond Bryan Brown, eds., *Professor in the Pulpit* (Nashville: Broadman Press, 1963) 6–7.

Much of the sermon deals with the ministry and personal tragedies of Don Harbuck—brilliant pastor, able preacher, Baptist theologian, and close friend. At twenty-one he had polio, and it left his arms paralyzed. Despite his handicap, he acquired a doctor's degree in theology, was a caring husband and father, and served as minister of significant Southern Baptist congregations.

In 1982, his wife, on whom he depended heavily because of his infirmity, died. Sometime after this loss, he planned to remarry. While waiting for the wedding, he was diagnosed as having an inoperable brain tumor. He nevertheless continued to preach as his condition allowed, and in one sermon Harbuck took as his text: "When I am weak I am strong" (2 Cor. 12:10).

In such adversity, ameliorated only by a sturdy faith, St. Amant finds an insight for the Christian. It is embodied in the words of the Apostle Paul: "My grace is sufficient, for my strength is displayed in weakness." Although human explanation is not adequate, there is a spiritual vitality to be found here. In the application of this truth to personal tragedy, genuine heroes of faith are created. Don Harbuck is a good example. St. Amant then added the exhortation of George Buttrick, the teacher of preachers and of preaching: "Pain is still a mystery. Lay hold on God in the time of suffering even if your grasp is no stronger than a prayer. You will find that God has already laid hold on you."[8]

St. Amant's understanding of the anxieties and challenges of what constitutes life for most of us is beautifully depicted in his sermon entitled "Turning Corners."[9] His primary text is Psalm 59:10a which he translates, "My God in his loving kindness shall meet me at every corner."

He proceeds to describe some of the "corners" of life we shall have to turn, and he shows how the Christian faith can give us confidence to face each crisis. The first "corner" is the new and unexpected, as when the child leaves the security of home to go to school, or one takes a new job, or new circumstances arise to which adjustment is difficult.

The second "corner" we face is the decision about what we are going to do with our lives. The third "corner" is the decision about marriage. The fourth "corner" he alludes to is what happens when our hopes fail, and the last "corner" is the fact of death.

This sermon not only identifies the critical experiences in life, but it is an eloquent reminder of God's presence at every pivotal stage of life. The psalmist says, "My God in his loving kindness shall meet me at every corner." "The corner of sorrow; the corner of temptation; the corner of pain; the corner of death, the last corner of all."

Preaching in the early 1960s, St. Amant emphasized the need for Christian discipleship. One powerful composition is entitled "Two Crosses," and

---

[8]Manuscript of sermon preached on 7 July 1984.
[9]Several texts are cited: Ps 23; Jer 1:8; Matt 28:18–20; Ps 59:10a.

the scriptural text is Matthew 16:21–26. In it he contrasts the passion of Communists with the indifference of many Christians. Although he allows for some exaggeration on both sides in this characterization, he adds, "and yet, who can deny that as Christians we are unduly preoccupied with comfort, conformity, and security. The values of our society are too much our own values, and these are material values."[10] He charged that the church is too timid, and he cites the warning of Dean William Inge:

> We are losing our Christianity because Christianity is a creed for heroes, and we are harmless, good-natured, little people who want everybody to have a good time.

What is needed is a return to the cross with its demand for genuine discipleship. Real discipleship requires participation both in Christ's death and Christ's resurrection, such as is seen in Dietrich Bonhoeffer who was martyred by the Nazis because he insisted on being faithful to the gospel.

St. Amant's preaching is marked by a genuine sophistication and a remarkable ability to communicate clearly, cogently, and even compellingly. His sermons add light and freshness to the subject he treats, and they are never dull, insipid, or trite. They give evidence of broad reading, wide interests, a sparkling imagination, and careful preparation. As preacher, he draws easily on poetry, plays, biography, history, travel, sports, current events, and personal observation to illuminate and explain the biblical text or narrative.

Furthermore, he possesses the rare gift of being able to find and state the essence of an idea or issue or complex problem—to reach the heart of the matter and to describe it in concise and understandable English. He uses his marvelous command of language and ideas to articulate a challenge to his audience to do better, to be better, to awaken to the opportunities of service, to live in an exemplary manner, to be sensitive to human needs, to overcome the difficulties and disappointments of life, and to be aware of God's wonderful world.

Although his sermons may cite the tragedies of the human experience and allude to the shortcomings of human behavior, there is almost always a note of hope, of encouragement, and of optimism to be found. This characteristic is not to be traced to mere sentimentality but to St. Amant's understanding of the nature of the gospel. It condemns sin and it calls for repentance, but that results in new possibilities, new resources, a new outlook, and a new relationship with God through Jesus Christ.

St. Amant has demonstrated his ability to interpret our times and the moods of society. An astute observer of American culture, he has pointed to its weaknesses, its fallacies, its presuppositions, and its threats to faith. He has reminded us that culture too is under Christ's judgment.

---

[10] Sermon manuscript entitled "Two Crosses."

In reviewing a large number of St. Amant's sermons, it is clear that several notes are sounded and recur with some frequency. There is a genuine concern over the impact which secularism has had on the modern mind and how Christian answers and solutions have been set aside and ignored. St. Amant's interest in the relation of culture to the Christian faith has documented this discontinuity.

The doctrines of sin and grace are stressed and are viewed as central to the gospel because they focus on man's condition and his potential. Too often, sin is rationalized and denied, and God's grace is consequently seen as irrelevant. At the heart of the gospel is the incarnation for the ultimate purpose of man's redemption.

St. Amant has a profound appreciation for those who have struggled to overcome life's obstacles and reverses. Such examples of faith and courage provide inspiration to others. In fact, their heroism in the face of personal suffering and immeasurable odds offers a model and a challenge to the rest of us.

St. Amant's sermons reveal a fine grasp of what a sermon ought to be. They are discourses on carefully defined themes; they have structure, progression, illustrations, humor, and biblical truth woven together; and they are delivered in such a way as to result in illumination, inspiration, and commitment. Furthermore, his sermons are usually marked by hope, optimism, broad sympathies, and a fascination with the remarkable ability of human beings to overcome the hurdles and handicaps of life. Found in his sermons, too, is a challenge to achieve, to overcome, and even to excel in the face of daunting odds and puzzling anomalies. A theme found in much of his preaching is, "There is hope in the midst of despair."

For a major part of his ministry as a seminary professor, St. Amant taught both church history and theology. Even after his teaching assignments led him more in the direction of church history, his interest in theology, its implications, and its trends continued and has been readily apparent. He is not only an historian but a theologian. As a consequence, his sermons, addresses, and articles reveal an intimate acquaintance with the views, the basic principles, and the writings of theologians. However, the technical terms and the jargon of theology have been studiously avoided as he has made a successful effort to communicate clearly and simply with his hearers.

St. Amant has often been called on to be the speaker on special occasions: to participate in the inauguration of a college president, to deliver a prestigious lecture series, to address a group of educators, or to preach in a college or seminary chapel for a special event or service. At such times he is at his best, whether proclaiming the Christian faith as preacher, analyzing the culture of our day, describing the Baptist heritage, or showing the relevance of the gospel for our times.

He has been particularly adept in demonstrating that the Christian faith has answers for man's questions, dilemmas, and frustrations. He often directs his sermons to man's intellectual search for meaning and his quest for personal maturity. The gospel he affirms and declares has potent resources to answer the fundamental questions of life.

In his many addresses delivered in an academic setting, St. Amant often has been expected to treat subjects dealing with the educational enterprise and the teaching profession. Because of five decades given to teaching, it is an area in which he has an extensive knowledge of the issues, leaders, bibliography, and competing philosophies. Consequently, he demonstrates an excellent grasp of the writings and perspectives of the shapers and spokesmen of American education as he alludes to their views and biases and influence. However, it should be added that his remarks to educators always bear the imprint of his own Christian convictions and commitment as he advocates the values of the Christian faith and seeks to relate those values to the educational process and the goals of learning. The basic themes of the New Testament are never neglected but are appropriately incorporated into the thrust of his assigned subject.

Even in his most scholarly sermons and addresses, St. Amant often makes reference to his favorite non-historical and non-ecclesiastical interest, namely, sports.

In an address presented at the inauguration of this writer at Georgetown College in 1984, he began by citing a story from the sports pages of the *Louisville Courier-Journal* which referred to "those tough Baptists from Georgetown College." It was a reference to the Georgetown Tigers football team, but he adapted the description and applied it to those "tough Baptists" who had founded the school more than 150 years earlier and to those who had kept it alive during the hard times in its history. Needless to say, this introduction cemented the attention of his hearers on the discourse which followed.

Not only has he had a love affair with sports, he is well aware that many who listen are sports fans too. He expertly uses a well-turned analogy or lesson drawn from athletic competition to illuminate a point or to supply an illustration. His sermon, "How Tall Is a Giant?," initially delivered in the chapel of Southern Baptist Seminary, is an excellent example of this very effective homiletic technique.

CONCLUSION

Although he has been much in demand by churches to preach for services of worship and to speak on special occasions, St. Amant's primary vehicle and forum for communicating the gospel has been the academic setting, and the classroom in particular. Thousands of students have been the beneficiaries of his pithy comments, his personal testimony, his appreciation of the best of the past, his keen sense of humor, and his optimism that a better world is possible through the appropriation and practice of the truths of the gospel. His lectures have been filled with theological insights and reminders of what is fundamentally important in life, namely, faith, hope, and love. But add to those Pauline virtues another triad, namely, a vision of what the future can be, a friendly tolerance and respect of other viewpoints, and an abiding appreciation for the wonderful world God has made.

Sometimes St. Amant has preached about the radiance of personal faith and the need to maintain it or to recover it when it has been lost. In such cases, he has suggested,

> we must return far oftener than we do to the central things, to the cross and to the empty tomb. We must ponder this gospel, this good news. Let us see anew the length of it; the loveliness of it; the majesty of it; the piercing pity of it; the searching challenge of it.[11]

As a preacher of the gospel, St. Amant has effectively, persuasively, insightfully, and comprehensively declared the Good News of Jesus Christ and that "the Gospel is the power of God unto salvation to everyone who believes."

---

[11] Sermon manuscript entitled "What Do You See?" with texts taken from Gen 13:1–15 and 2 Cor 4:1–6.

C. PENROSE ST. AMANT: INTERPRETER OF THE BAPTIST VISION

WALTER B. SHURDEN
Mercer University, Macon GA 31207

Since being a first year seminary student in the late 1950s, I have been a "St. Amant watcher" and a "St. Amant reader." Although I never had a formal academic course with him, I have watched him preach, lecture and speak on special occasions numerous times. Incidentally, St. Amant, as Frank Stagg suggests, is one of those people you need to see and hear speak before you read. Once you have seen and heard him speak you cannot possibly read him without envisioning how he would have spoken it.

For the last thirty years I have also been an avid St. Amant reader. What he thinks on any subject, including something as mundane as Denny Crum's Louisville Cardinals basketball team, matters to me. His book reviews, for example, have always been of particular interest.

St. Amant has balance without blandness. And that, as much as anything else, is why I and many others have watched and read him for three to four decades. My image of St. Amant is that of a tight-rope artist who "leans," but only very, very slightly, to the left, always maintaining his balance. In fact, about the time you think he is "leaning" left, he slightly and carefully shifts to the right, never for safety but for comprehensiveness. St. Amant balance is part personality but it is also part recognition that ambiguities exceed simplistic explanations.

A casual reading of the articles in this volume reflects what I am calling the "St. Amant balance." Stagg interpreted St. Amant's vocational move toward administration in light of "gifts for bringing people together, respecting their diversities and maximizing their commonalities."[1] Reflecting on St. Amant's successful ten year deanship at Southern Seminary, Glenn Hinson said:

> St. Amant manifested throughout his administration a remarkable feeling for *the right balance* of concerns: the denomination and the world of theological education, professional and graduate education, faculty and administration, students and faculty, church and society.[2]

Keith Parker, writing about St. Amant as President of Rüschlikon, echoed the same theme: "Penrose St. Amant . . . was a 'bridging' president, one whose gifts and unique leadership actually bridged the past, present and fu-

---

[1] Above, p. 22.

[2] Above, p. 50.

ture, as well as the multiple cultures and tasks the seminary faced."[3] More succinctly, Parker said of St. Amant that he was "always seeking a balance or healthy tension between inevitable opposites."[4]

But underscore this—in red, if necessary! In St. Amant, balance never meant blandness. Nothing could be further from Penrose St. Amant than the historian who hides behind the security of uninterpreted data. St. Amant has a point of view. The fact that it is expressed almost always calmly and in a dialectic neither washes out nor waters down perspective.

Nowhere does St. Amant's dialectical approach manifest itself more clearly than in his description of the Baptist identity. His interpretation of the Baptist vision is far more than an academic exercise in historical research; it is a life commitment based on a historical movement, but it is almost always expressed in polarities. Based upon his published articles, the following is what I see as his primary emphases in profiling the Baptist identity.

"AN OPEN BIBLE AND AN OPEN MIND"

"An open Bible and an open mind" is Penrose St. Amant's succinct summary for what being a Baptist means. Indeed, his essential vision of the Baptist way is wrapped up in this phrase, so repetitious in his writings. He used the line in almost every article he wrote concerning the Baptist heritage.[5]

Why is he so fond of the phrase and what does he mean by it? He utilized the phrase because he believes that at the heart of the Baptist vision is a dynamic tension, a taut dialectic which is not subject to a singular and simplistic reductionism. The dialectic St. Amant addresses with the phrase is, of course, that of authority and freedom within the Baptist tradition. Synonyms for the St. Amant slogan pour from the professor's pen. They look like this:

Open Bible	Open Mind
Authority	Freedom
Lordship of Christ	Soul Competency
Unity	Diversity
Loyalty	Liberty
Conviction	Tolerance
Biblical Faith	Believer's Freedom
Core	Periphery
Continuity	Change
Certainty	Mystery

---

[3] Above, p. 53.

[4] Above, p. 61.

[5] See, for example, the following articles by St. Amant: "Our Baptist Heritage," *The Quarterly Review* 10:3 (July-August-September 1950): 19; "Other Baptist Bodies," *Baptist Advance*, Davis Collier Woolley, ed. (Nashville: Broadman, 1964) 368; "Our Baptist Heritage and the Church," *Baptist History and Heritage* 2:2 (July 1967): 88; "Southern Baptists: Unity in Diversity," *Search* 1:3 (Spring 1971): 13; "Baptist Pluralism and Unity," *Baptists and The American Experience*, James E. Wood, Jr. ed. (Valley Forge: Judson, 1976) 353; "Perspectives in our Baptist Heritage," *Discovering Our Baptist Heritage*, William H. Brackney, ed. (Valley Forge: The American Baptist Historical Society, 1985) 11.

In my judgment, St. Amant's most mature, thorough and philosophical statement of the Baptist tradition is found in "Baptist Pluralism and Unity," an appropriately titled essay for St. Amant. He began the article by referring to the motto on the Great Seal of the United States—*E Pluribus Unum*. Throughout the article St. Amant hammered away at the idea that the motto enunciated an important element in the Baptist heritage. He concluded the article with the following paragraph:

> *E Pluribus Unum* (out of many, one) is not a static goal toward which we strive but a dynamic process that goes on and on. This motto does not pose a problem we hope one day to solve. For Baptists, it is a way of life.[6]

For St. Amant, being Baptist means "a creative balance between conservation and change." Two basic tendencies mark the Baptist heritage, he said. They are "the unity that flows from our belief that God has spoken and speaks in his Word and the diversity that flows from our freedom to listen, to read, and to implement what we hear."[7]

With somewhat different language, St. Amant echoed the open Bible-open mind, unity-in-diversity theme in his most recent statement of the Baptist identity. St. Amant wrote of "the two foci that stand at the center of the Baptist witness" and identified these as "Christ's lordship and the individual's conscience under God."[8] Later in the same article he referred to the polarity within the Baptist heritage as "the Biblical faith" and "the believer's freedom."[9]

An open Bible! That is crucial to St. Amant, partly because of his personal spiritual history, a history he later critiqued but never amputated. "The thing I remember most vividly about the small Baptist community in which I grew up in South Louisiana," he said, "is the ubiquity of Bibles which people not only displayed but read."[10] And St. Amant's mother, a Roman Catholic when she married, became a Baptist by reading the New Testament, an event St. Amant describes with warm appreciation.[11]

Personally, therefore, St. Amant is anchored to Holy Scripture. Unapologetically and straightforwardly he declares, "The Bible is the written Word of God."[12] This affirmation of religious authority is for St. Amant denominationally as well as personally rooted. "Baptists believe," he told the Baptist World Alliance, that "there is a sure Word from God which illuminates

---

[6]Penrose St. Amant, "Baptist Pluralism and Unity," 359.
[7]Ibid., 353.
[8]Penrose St. Amant, "Perspectives in our Baptist Heritage," 11.
[9]Ibid., 13.
[10]Ibid., 14.
[11]Penrose St. Amant, "The Teaching Church and Our Baptist Witness," *The Truth That Makes Men Free: Official Report of the Eleventh Congress of the Baptist World Alliance, Miami Beach, Florida, June 25–30, 1965*, Josef Nordenhaug, ed. (Nashville: Broadman, 1986) 350.
[12]"Southern Baptist Theology Today: An Interview with C. Penrose St. Amant," *The Theological Educator* 12:2 (Spring 1982): 17.

the meaning of our human pilgrimage and provides power and direction for the journey."[13] Biblical faith, he continued, cannot be contrived by people to suit themselves because it "comes to us out of the mighty events in Scripture, which bears a divine revelation." The substance and sustaining power of the Baptist witness is this "emphasis on the Bible as the norm of faith and practice."[14]

St. Amant's contention for "the open Bible" in Baptist life also has a serious philosophical and theological dimension to it. He fears the exclusivistic claims of fundamentalists based upon narrow and dogmatic assertions, but he also winces at the inclusivistic claims of liberals based upon theological relativism.[15] Here, again, is the taut dialectic.

St. Amant points out that serious consequences flow from a purely relativistic view of the world. Relativism breeds skepticism! And skepticism creates a philosophical vacuum from which new absolutist claims emerge. "The contemporary world, therefore," he said in 1982, "is ripe for the proliferation of cults, the resurgence of fundamentalism, and a renewed liberalism, all of which offer simplistic solutions to the complicated problems of today's world."[16] Pluralism, while always a revered virtue by St. Amant, can be pushed, he argued toward atomism. The result is not a creative diversity but a brokenness, isolationism and alienation. This disintegration of authority is often accompanied by the cultivation of naked power. Baptists, therefore, must have and have had, according to St. Amant, a center and core. The Baptist center is the open Bible.

Penrose St. Amant is not personally, theologically or denominationally capable, however, of speaking of the open Bible as the unity of Baptist life without simultaneously affirming the open mind as the source of diversity among Baptists. Just as the biblical faith creates Baptist loyalty, believer's freedom promotes Baptist liberty. In one of his earliest articles on the Baptist identity, St. Amant suggested that while the open Bible had saved Baptists from a superficial secularism, the open mind had saved them from a narrow sectarianism.[17] Of course, St. Amant recognized that Baptists had at times indeed been entrapped by both secularism and sectarianism. Within the Baptist genius, however, were antidotes to these twin demons.

The open mind! Why has St. Amant insisted upon it as integral to the Baptist identity? Because of his incurable penchant for balance? Yes, that is part of the answer. Because of his belief that today's unchecked authority becomes tomorrow's insufferable tyranny? Yes, that is another part of it. In ad-

---

[13]"The Teaching Church and Our Baptist Witness," 346.
[14]Ibid., 350.
[15]"Baptist Pluralism and Unity," 355.
[16]"Southern Baptist Theology Today: An Interview with C. Penrose St. Amant," 21.
[17]"Our Baptist Heritage," 19.

dition to these more obvious and generic reasons for coupling freedom with authority and liberty with loyalty, St. Amant, I think, saw at least three other origins of diversity among Baptists.

One is biblical. An "open mind" is made necessary by the clear biblical teaching of diversity of gifts.[18] Primarily because he is historically and theologically oriented by academic training, St. Amant did not use this biblical argument as often or as thoroughly as he used others. In his last major description of the Baptist identity, however, he wrote explicitly of the one *charisma* (Rom 6:23) and the variety of *charismata* (1 Cor 12:7 and Rom 12:3ff.), the latter to be used for the common good of the Body of Christ. The variety of gifts must find free expression among Baptists and that occurs only where openness to diversity and individual conscience is honored.

According to St. Amant, the "open mind" is also made mandatory for a theological reason, and that is human selfishness. Baptists, he avers, have emphasized both "the sanctity and the sinfulness" of all people, including Baptists. And then he adds in Niebuhrian fashion, "Our philosophy of diversity, rooted in a basic respect for the individual conscience and in the recognition of the taint of self-interest in our judgments of what is just and true, is one of the threads that paradoxically binds us together."[19] Precisely because our vision of what is true and right is human and incredibly tainted by self-interest, we need "the corrective of competing visions."[20] An "open mind" is mandated by human sin.

A third reason for an "open mind" is cultural. The diversity in Baptist life and thought is merely a reflection of the "particular histories, races, nationalities, background, sections, and cultural and educational levels" expressed within and by the numerous Baptist groups in the United States and around the world.[21] It is a "mistake" to promote a Baptist melting-pot where diversities are neutralized. Even if it were possible, said St Amant, the cancellation of Baptist differences in the hope of an abstract model of unity would be undesirable.[22] The preacher in the historian is unrestrained as he describes Baptist diversity in music (from Fanny Crosby to Beethoven), in preaching (from George W. Truett to Harold Cooke Phillips), and in worship (from New Zion Baptist Church in rural Mississippi to the colorful liturgy of Myers Park Baptist Church in Charlotte, North Carolina).

What specifically does the "open mind" half of St. Amant's Baptist dialectic mean? His applications of the phrase to Baptist life are varied and nu-

---

[18]"Perspectives in Our Baptist Heritage," 12; "Southern Baptists: Unity in Diversity," 7.

[19]"Baptist Pluralism and Unity," 352.

[20]Ibid., 358; see also "Southern Baptists: Unity in Diversity," 8.

[21]"Perspectives in Our Baptist Heritage," 14.

[22]"Baptist Pluralism and Unity," 354.

merous. He applies it, for example, to the study of the Bible, calling Baptists to embrace fearlessly biblical criticism.[23] One of his most repeated applications, however, of the "open mind" is to the *interpretation* of the Bible. It is in this connection that he is reminiscent of E.Y. Mullins's affirmation that "soul competency" is the centerpiece of Baptist theology. Writing in the midst of the Broadman controversy when fundamentalist Southern Baptists were seeking to impose their peculiar interpretation of the Bible on others, St. Amant called on Baptists to be Baptists:

> The final arbiter of what the Bible means for Baptists is not the biblical scholar, nor the pastor, nor the editor of this or that, nor a consensus of the Southern Baptist Convention, nor the so-called liberal or conservative or moderate by whatever definitions. We do not believe in the authority of popes or synods or conventions or associations or churches or pastors or professors over the individual conscience. *Either we take seriously the competency of the individual in this matter or we do not. And if we do not, we repudiate in one full swoop an essential element in our Baptist heritage.* Diversity among us is the result of what has been called soul competency.[24]

In another place, St. Amant related soul competency to the Baptist doctrine of the priesthood of believers which carries with it the "right of Christians to read, study, and interpret the Bible and the responsibility to observe what it teaches."[25]

So the "open mind" means for St. Amant the legitimation of a serious scholarly study of the Bible and the necessity of the individual to be free to interpret the Bible. And because creedalism ends up with an imposed uniformity and operates on the basis of a "closed mind," St. Amant often applied his "open mind" category to a vigorous anti-creedalism. As a historian of the Christian church, St. Amant knows that creedalism is both divisive and ineffective; theological unity cannot come from prescribed faith which is then imposed. Being biblical rather than creedal, St. Amant said, "Baptists have no leader who cannot be challenged in the name of truth and have no confession of faith that cannot be challenged on the basis of the Bible."[26] Speaking in the midst of the inerrancy controversy, when fundamentalists again were seeking to creedalize uniformity through "The Baptist Faith and Message," St. Amant reminded Southern Baptists, "We have never been a creedal people and we had better not start now."[27] For St. Amant, an "open mind" said "yes" to biblical authority but "no" to creedalism.

---

[23]"Southern Baptist Theology Today: An Interview with C. Penrose St. Amant," 16, 17.

[24]"Southern Baptists: Unity in Diversity," 6. The underlining is mine for emphasis.

[25]Penrose St. Amant, "Some Resources for Reconciliation in Our Baptist Heritage," *Baptist Heritage Update* 2:1 (Spring 1986): 5.

[26]"Southern Baptist Theology Today: An Interview with C. Penrose St. Amant," 29.

[27]Ibid., 27.

An "open mind," as St. Amant developed it, has two pastoral dimensions. One, open-mindedness, is related to charitable attitudes. St. Amant quoted often an 1802 "circular letter" distributed by a Kentucky association. The "Dear Brethren" to whom the letter was addressed were warned "to watch against a spirit of dogmatical Arrogance and Bigotry."[28]

St. Amant also pointed out that Baptist freedom meant we should major on majors, not on minors. He enjoyed telling of the boat pilot who regularly plied the Mississippi River. Asked if he knew where the sandbars were, the pilot replied, "No, but I know where the channel is." St. Amant believed that the "open mind" would not dissipate its energies on bypaths and negations. It would focus on "majors" which unite, not "minors" which divide.[29]

Like John Clifford, E. Y. Mullins, George W. Truett and other Baptist leaders before him, St. Amant is totally aware of the dangers of freedom and the "open mind." "Freedom can be a cloak for license and subversion," he confessed. But then he quickly added, "but the glory . . . of the Baptists is that we believe the dangers of freedom are much less than the dangers of tyranny."[30]

A PERSONAL FAITH AND A PUBLIC WITNESS

It has now long since become a shibboleth to assert the need for a personal and a public faith. The fact of the matter, however, as Martin Marty has demonstrated, is that American Christianity has been in a tug-of-war for years over which is the more important. So have Baptists. Penrose St. Amant, through his preaching, lecturing and writing has called Baptists to both commitments. He believes it necessary, if Baptists are to be faithful to what it means to be Baptist, that they refuse to choose one or the other but affirm both at the same time. Unfortunately, St. Amant's single best treatment of this subject remains unpublished,[31] but many of his published writings address the subject. Concerning this dialectic of personal versus social faith, let us begin with a description of the "St. Amant balance" again!

> "We are on a two-way street. If we start with the gospel for society, we run into the need for better people who alone can create and sustain a creative social order; and, therefore, we face the personal gospel. If we start with the

---

[28]"Perspectives in Our Baptist Heritage," 18; "Baptist Pluralism and Unity," 352; "Southern Baptists: Unity in Diversity," 13.

[29]"Southern Baptists: Unity in Diversity," 12; see also "Our Baptist Heritage," 19.

[30]C. Penrose St. Amant, "Baptist Heritage and Religious Liberty," *The Quarterly Review* 23:2 (April-May-June 1963): 20.

[31]Penrose St. Amant, "A Historical View of Baptist Involvement in Citizenship," an unpublished address presented to the Christian Citizenship Seminar in Washington, D. C., sponsored by the Christian Life Commission of the Southern Baptist Convention, 23 March 1964.

personal gospel, we run into social structures which thwart personal creativity; and, therefore, we face the gospel for society. There is really only one gospel. This gospel promises forgiveness of sins, but also enjoins our responsibility for the welfare of the neighbors.[32]

Several years ago W. R. White wrote a book entitled *Baptist Distinctives,* including a chapter on "The Primacy of the Individual." Before White, E. Y. Mullins wrote in *The Axioms of Religion* of "the principle of individualism in religion." Before Mullins, John Clifford spoke of "sanctified individualism" as a major attribute of the Baptists. St. Amant follows in their train. Without ignoring the community of the church, he, nevertheless, highlights the individual and the personal aspects of faith.

In his most systematic statement of the corporate demands of the gospel, St. Amant began, significantly, with a section on "Christian Conversion," because "the starting point of the Christian life is when God invades human life redemptively in Jesus Christ."[33] In an inspiring sermon before the 1975 Baptist World Congress, he quoted H. G. Wells who, after cataloging human achievements, concluded by saying that humans continue to behave like quarrelsome apes. Wells's simplistic remedy was "stop being an ape." To which St. Amant responded soteriologically:

> Well, more than this is required. What is required is not a pat on the back, a shot in the arm, a bit of eyewash to make the world look better. What is required is a drastic human transformation, a new birth, a new creation. . . .[34]

His soteriology, underlying the necessity of the personal appropriation of divine grace for human "apeness," is related also to St. Amant's Baptist understanding of epistemology, ecclesiology and missiology. At the close of an interview on contemporary Southern Baptist theology, St. Amant said, "Throughout our conversation, I have stressed the personal dimension of our pilgrimage, as Christians who have embraced the Baptist way." And then after elaborating upon Martin Buber's thesis in *I and Thou,* a very important book for St. Amant, he added, "A certain depth of understanding is available in no way other than through personal encounter."[35] His concept of how one knows (personal encounter) is a philosophical corollary to the theological question of how one becomes a Christian (personal faith). Here is the primacy of the personal, so basic to the Baptist identity.

---

[32]Penrose St. Amant, "Baptists in a Revolutionary Age," *Baptist History and Heritage* 7:3 (July 1972): 147.

[33]"A Historical View of Baptist Involvement in Citizenship," 1.

[34]Penrose St. Amant, "Are Christians Really New People?" *New People For A New World—Through Christ: Official Report of the Thirteenth Congress, Baptist World Alliance, Stockholm, Sweden, July 8–13, 1975,* Cyril E. Bryant, ed. (Nashville: Broadman, 1976) 52.

[35]"Southern Baptist Theology Today: An Interview with C. Penrose St. Amant," 30.

Baptist ecclesiology, erected upon the concept of a believer's church, cannot be understood apart from the vibrant personal faith of individuals, said St. Amant.[36] Likewise, the expansion and growth of the Baptist witness was due to "the emphasis placed upon Christian experience." Baptist Christianity, with its emphasis on personal experience, is always on the verge of asking, "If it be not light to me, what care I how light it be?"[37] Experientialism has been historically basic to the Baptist profile; it is also fundamental for Penrose St. Amant.

But just as Christ is Saviour in an intensely experiential and personal way, he is also Lord in a profoundly social and public way. The Baptist vision of Christianity, says St. Amant, pulls its adherents inexorably into the corporate realm. The theological foundation on which the public witness rests for Baptists is the Lordship of Christ.

How does the Lordship of Christ, "a theme familiar to Baptists," impact our public witness? St. Amant's writings suggest three ways. First, the Lordship of Christ challenges all idolatries. In St. Amant's language, "it offers a counterpoise to the tendency of man to sacralize his own words."[38] Because "we have no Lord but Christ . . . no one else and nothing else can command the final allegiance of our lives."[39] Such a theological conviction may in one instance breed revolution when confronted by the idolatry of status quo. But in another instance it rejects revolution that seeks to usurp the rule of Christ in the life of the individual and church. The Christian and the church are obligated to desacralize contemporary gods, placing them under the Lordship of Christ.

Second, the Lordship of Christ challenges the passivity and inactivity of Christians. St. Amant has no time for the gnosticism which denies history or the pietism which ignores history. To establish a dichotomy between the secular and the sacred "has no basis either in the New Testament or in Baptist history."[40] The Baptist conscience, political freedom, the plight of the common person, and the democratic process have all acted to drive Baptists, however reluctantly, into the world with their word of witness.

Third, the Lordship of Christ also challenges human despair. Fatalism is heresy for disciples of Christ. "We can't do anything about it," is simply not a proper response for people who view the pain and injustice of the world through the eyes of the Nazarene. Although potent, the principalities and powers of the world are not omnipotent. Public witness, therefore, is a requirement of discipleship according to St. Amant.[41]

---

[36]"Perspectives in Our Baptist Heritage," 12.
[37]"Our Baptist Heritage," 19.
[38]"Baptists in a Revolutionary Age," 146.
[39]Ibid.
[40]"A Historical View of Baptist Involvement in Citizenship," 1.
[41]"Baptists in a Revolutionary Age," 146.

When interpreting the Baptist way, St. Amant often addressed specific social issues such as race,[42] international disarmament,[43] and support for public education.[44] More often than not, however, St. Amant utilized the Baptist heritage to confront "secularism" and "Culture Christianity." The terms, which could be treated separately, are often used interchangeably by the professor.

In one of his most provocative and persuasive articles,[45] St. Amant confronted the burgeoning secularism in American life with a stubborn insistence on the Baptist ideal of voluntarism. Published in 1963, St. Amant's article came out shortly after *Engel v. Vitale* (1962) and about the time of *Abington School District v. Schempp* (1963). In the first decision the Supreme Court prohibited, under the "no establishment" clause of the First Amendment, a prayer drafted by the New York Board of Regents. In the second decision, the Court forbade the devotional reading of the Bible in tax-supported schools.

These rulings, so symbolic of secularism, caused consternation among many of the religious in America. Some were so frightened that they began to question the effectiveness of the voluntary principle in American life. Indeed, some Protestant churchmen began to use the traditional Roman Catholic argument that the villain was the honored doctrine of the separation of church and state. The steeple was ringing for help from the courthouse!

St. Amant recognized the reality of a growing secularism, but he refused to believe "that we must repudiate the great tradition of the American churches,"[46] or the cardinal Baptist affirmation of the separation of church and state. Reminding Baptists of their past commitment to the separation of church and state, St. Amant warned of the future, "We must be vigilant, not only must we oppose encroachments upon this principle, we must prove to the world that the voluntary principle in religion . . . can produce a radiant and powerful faith.[47]

The demise of the wall of separation, St. Amant screamed, would mean not simply the secularization of American culture but more importantly secularization of American churches! What government supports, government regulates! The solution to secularism was not for weak churches to seek help from the muscles of government, but to strengthen homes and churches, the

---

[42]"A Historical View of Baptist Involvement in Citizenship," 9; see also, "Southern Baptists and Southern Culture," *Review and Expositor* 67:2 (Spring 1970): 150.

[43]Penrose St. Amant, "Communicating the Gospel in the Eighties," *The Quarterly Review* 41:3 (April-May-June 1981): 70, 71.

[44]Penrose St. Amant, "Baptists and Public Education: An Historical Perspective," *The Quarterly Review* 44:2 (January-February-March 1984): 66–78.

[45]"Baptist Heritage and Religious Liberty," 16–21.

[46]Ibid., 17.

[47]Ibid., 18.

citadels of faith, and to affirm and accept the "grave responsibilities" of religious liberty.

Just as St. Amant used the Baptist principle of voluntarism against a pervasive secularism, so did he draw from the Baptist heritage to combat what he called "culture Christianity." A lover of art, music and literature, Penrose St. Amant was certainly not deprecating "culture" in that sense of the word. "Culture Christianity" was for him faith shorn of the prophetic. "Culture Christianity" could escape the prophetic dimensions of the Christian faith by retreating into private virtues or by equating public Christian responsibility with specific political, economic or ideological reform movements. Baptists, St. Amant believed, had not always avoided "Culture Christianity," but they had resources in the Baptist arsenal to steer them away from it. These resources, he said,

> involve a strong evangelical emphasis upon conversion with an equally strong stress upon Christian ethics, both in an individual and a corporate sense. They involve an awareness of the subtlety and pervasiveness of sin and the wondrous depths of grace. They involve regenerate lives which issue in disciplined and disciplining communities that have the audacity to seek to revolutionize human history. Our heritage brings together a certain biblical realism, a passionate concern for Christian experience, a sensitivity to the moral and spiritual dimensions of civilization, a suspicion of too much power in the hands of too few people, a fierce dedication to freedom, and a profound sense of destiny under God.[48]

After analyzing St. Amant's published statements on the general subject of the Baptist heritage and social responsibility one discovers St. Amant speaking in various roles. St. Amant the historian described what Baptists have and have not done and why. With his emphasis on the Lordship of Christ, St. Amant the theologian provided biblical foundation for action. St. Amant the prophet predicted consequences for failure to act. But St. Amant the preacher called for Baptists to care, to move through life compassionately, to participate in the meaning of the cross. He enjoyed quoting Baron Friedrich von Hügel's dying words, "Caring is everything; nothing matters but caring."[49]

DENOMINATIONAL ROOTS AND ECUMENICAL COMMITMENTS

In Walker Percy's *The Second Coming*, Will Barrett left his native South in order to get away "from the ancient hatred and allegiances" of his father. He even tried to believe in the Christian God because his father did not. Will exclaimed, "Imagine having to leave the South to find God!" Penrose St.

---

[48] "Baptists in a Revolutionary Age," 153.
[49] "Our Baptist Heritage and the Church," 89, 90, 113. See also Penrose St. Amant, "Is History Made by Heroes?" *Baptist History and Heritage* 1:1 (August 1965): 55.

Amant has refused to believe that God could not be found in the South or among Southern Baptists. On the other hand, he never perceived of God as a Southern Baptist monopoly. His religious roots run deeply and affectionately into Southern Baptist soil, but geography and denomination do not by any means exhaust his understanding of the universal Church of Jesus Christ. St. Amant is denominationally rooted and ecumenically committed.

In a moving, autobiographical statement, St. Amant told of his appreciation for the church of his past.

> My earliest memory of the church is a small congregation worshipping in a modest frame building in a predominantly Roman Catholic village in south Louisiana. The wooden, cushionless benches were always hard, the sermons often long, and my mother's lap inviting. Often I went to sleep shortly after the sermon started and was usually awakened by the singing of a rousing gospel song. And yet what happened there was so meaningful that at the age of seven I made a public profession of faith in Christ, was baptized, and began to participate in the life of the church, a community of folk for whom Jesus Christ was Saviour and Lord. Upon its deepest level, whatever else the church means, it still means this to me.

And then he added,

> The New Testament and our Baptist heritage have tended to confirm my childhood memories. It seems to me that the church is essentially a simpler fact than many church historians have made it. Is it not true that the gathering together of a local congregation of believers, the breaking of bread, prayers, and the worship of Jesus Christ, the Lord, is the oldest ecclesiastical fact in Christendom?[50]

"That little church in which I was nurtured," St. Amant believed, is also the "little church that lies at the heart of our Baptist heritage."[51] And at the heart of "that little church" were "plain people." St. Amant was fond of historian Robert Torbet's appraisal of Baptists in America. Torbet said that in the century following the Great Awakening Baptists were characterized by "a strong appeal to the plain people of the agrarian areas."[52]

One of St. Amant's strengths as an interpreter of the Baptist vision is that, despite his background of some privilege, he knew and appreciated the fact that Baptists were "plain people." "The Baptist movement," he said, "has always remained close to the common people,"[53] and that fact accounts for

---

[50]"Our Baptist Heritage and the Church," 83.

[51]"Perspectives in our Baptist Heritage," 14.

[52]For examples of St. Amant's use of this phrase, see, "A Historical View of Baptist Involvement in Citizenship," 10; "Southern Baptists and Southern Culture," 151; "Baptists in a Revolutionary Age," 153.

[53]"Our Baptist Heritage," 18.

the remarkable growth of Baptists in America. St. Amant's respect for "plain people" and his emphasis on the priesthood of all believers served to reenforce each other, especially in the area of biblical interpretation. As a theological professor, dean and president, St. Amant certainly never discounted or minimized the crucial role of the professional scholar in biblical interpretation, but neither did his life of scholarly pursuits ever blur his denominational vision that "a cardinal Baptist teaching is that the Bible should *not* be left to the experts alone but should be put into the hands of the people."[54] In the same vein, St. Amant lobbied for "a closer relationship between our theological seminaries and the people in the churches who make the seminaries possible by their support."[55]

Even in the light of his world travels—his education in Scotland and France and his seminary presidency in Switzerland—St. Amant, in one sense, never left home. While never militantly defensive he could get testy over accusations, misinterpretations and distortions of both his native South and his Southern Baptist heritage.[56] He placed in suspect, for example, the notion that Southern Baptists were simply a religious expression of Southern culture. His education and broad experience certainly set St. Amant free from the restrictive parochialisms of his past, but he was never set adrift on a sea of ingratitude.

But he had been set free! If he "never left home" in one sense, in a paradoxical sense he refused to stay home. He, for example, like most Southern Baptist scholars of his generation, had been liberated from the haughty Landmarkism in Southern Baptist life which insisted that the local church is the only church. "The genius of our heritage," he confessed, "is that the church at its best is both the body of Christ and the gathered community at the same time."[57]

St. Amant saw clearly a dangerous sectarianism in Southern Baptist life. He saw it in our unnecessary separation from the mainstream of Protestantism, in our reluctance to enter the ecumenical dialogue,[58] in our distorted emphasis on the local church,[59] in our biblical primitivism which ignores church history in general[60] and in our defensive denominational historiography which tells our story as though it occurred in a cultural vacuum.[61]

---

[54]"Perspectives in our Baptist Heritage," 14.

[55]"Southern Baptist Theology Today: An Interview with C. Penrose St. Amant," 29.

[56]See for example, "Southern Baptists and Southern Culture," 144; and C. Penrose St. Amant, "Our Task," *Baptist History and Heritage* 1:2 (July 1966): 5.

[57]"Our Baptist Heritage and the Church," 85.

[58]"Baptists in a Revolutionary Age," 151.

[59]"Southern Baptist Theology Today: An Interview," 27.

[60]"Perspectives in our Baptist Heritage," 16.

[61]"Southern Baptists and Southern Culture," 144–46.

Concerning the Baptist heritage and the larger Christian heritage, Penrose St. Amant called, characteristically, for balance, what he described as "a certain dialectical attitude." He wrote,

> To escape the posture of claiming too much for ourselves as Baptists, we do not need to abandon our heritage. We do not need to give up our roots and embrace the unreality of Christianity in general to deal with our sectarianism. We do need a discriminating reappraisal of our heritage now so that it becomes not a bastion to be defended but an instrument which carries our vision of the gospel in company with Christian comrades shaped by other histories. We have much to give and much to learn. Let's do both.[62]

CONCLUSION

If space had permitted, I would have developed one other dialectic, not so much about St. Amant's interpretation of the Baptist vision (though certainly related) as about St. Amant himself. It would have been designated "Historical Consciousness and Contemporary Hope." He wrote often and passionately about Baptists' need to discuss and know their history. Within that history of voluntarism, freedom, religious liberty, "open Bibles," "open minds," and "plain people" were resources for guiding, inspiring and strengthening.

Although a student and lover of the past, Penrose St. Amant is essentially and fundamentally a forward looking person, optimistic and hopeful. In the broadest sense, his hope is based on the gospel, the good news of the life, death and resurrection of the Nazarene carpenter. In reading St. Amant, however, one comes away with the conviction that his hope is not unrelated to his Baptist heritage. The individualism of Baptist theology shapes St. Amant's hopefulness. He believes that one lonely soul can make a difference.[63] And maybe it was his "plain people" understanding of Baptist history that caused him to say that one does not have to do spectacular things to effect creative change.[64] Even in the face of secularism and the octopus-like arms of culture, squeezing the church at every point of its life, he continues to believe that life-transforming events occur in the "little church that lies at the heart of the Baptist heritage." Through most of his writing breathes the whisper, "the gates of hell shall not prevail."

---

[62] "Baptists in a Revolutionary Age," 151.
[63] "Our Task," 6.
[64] "Baptists in a Revolutionary Age," 142.

Penrose St. Amant, as the previous articles in this volume happily demonstrate, is no longer a mere interpreter of the Baptist heritage; he is now a part of that heritage. He has proved his maxim, rooted in his Baptist background, that one person can make a difference.

C. PENROSE ST. AMANT: A BIBLIOGRAPHY

LYNN E. MAY, JR.
Southern Baptist Historical Commission, Nashville TN 37203–3620

I. BOOKS, BOOKLETS, AND ESSAYS/ARTICLES IN BOOKS

St. Amant, C. Penrose, "Academic Freedom," in Davis C. Woolley, ed., vol. 3 of *Encyclopedia of Southern Baptists* (Nashville: Broadman Press, 1971) 1553.

──────. "Are Christians Really New People?" in *New People for A New World.* Report of Thirteenth Baptist World Congress (Nashville: Broadman Press, 1975) 49–53.

──────. "Baptist Pluralism and Unity," in James E. Wood, ed. *Baptists and the American Experience* (Valley Forge PA: Judson Press, 1976) 347–60.

──────. *Called to Serve, Called to Lead.* Address at the inauguration of W. Morgan Patterson as President of Georgetown College, 22 October 1984. (Georgetown KY: Georgetown College, 1984.)

──────. *Christian Faith and History.* Holland Foundation Lectures, 1954. (Ft. Worth TX: Southwestern Baptist Theological Seminary, 1954.)

──────. "Christian Faith Confronts the Modern Mind," in G. Paul Butler, ed., *Best Sermons, 1949–50* (New York: Harper and Brothers, 1951).

──────. "Christianity, History of," in Norman W. Cox, ed., vol. 1 of *Encyclopedia of Southern Baptists* (Nashville: Broadman Press, 1958) 262–69.

──────. *Christianity on the World's Frontiers.* Binns Lectures, William Jewell College, 17–19 February 1987. (Liberty MO: William Jewell College, 1987.)

──────. *The Church: A Community of Celebration.* A sermon at national meeting of Association of Clinical Pastoral Education, 7 September 1980. Published by Association of Clinical Pastoral Education, 1980.

──────. "The Ecumenical Movement and Protestantism's Future," in *We Hold These Truths* (Protestants and Other Americans United, 1964).

──────. Faith for Life. Series of radio messages.(New Orleans: New Orleans Baptist Theological Seminary, 1956.)

──────. "The First Sunday in Lent," in Horace A. Weaver, ed., *International Lesson Annual* (Nashville: Abingdon Press, 1966) 77–79.

──────. "Frontier, Baptists and the American," in Cox, vol. 1 of *Encyclopedia of Southern Baptists* (Nashville: Broadman Press, 1958) 510–12.

_____. *Historical Sketch of the Louisiana Baptist Student Union* (Alexandria LA: Department of Student Work, Louisiana Baptist Convention, 1956).

_____. *A History of the Presbyterian Church in Louisiana* (Richmond VA: Whittet and Shepperson, 1961).

_____. "How Tall Is a Giant?" in W. Morgan Patterson and Raymond B. Brown, *Professor in the Pulpit* (Nashville: Broadman Press, 1963).

_____. "Immaculate Conception," in Cox, vol. 1 of *Encyclopedia of Southern Baptists* (Nashville: Broadman Press, 1958) 676.

_____. *Isn't One Religion as Good as Another?* (Nashville: Student Department, Sunday School Board, SBC, 1958).

_____. "Louisiana," in Samuel S. Hill, ed., *Religion in the Southern States: A Historical Study* (Macon GA: Mercer University Press, 1983) 123–45.

_____. "Louisiana Baptist Convention, History of," in Cox, vol. 2 of *Encyclopedia of Southern Baptists* (Nashville: Broadman Press, 1958) 800–804.

_____. "Mass and Transubstantiation," in Cox, vol. 2 of *Encyclopedia of Southern Baptists* ((Nashville: Broadman Press, 1958) 835–36.

_____. "The New Church History," in E. J. Vardaman and J. Leo Garrett, Jr., eds. *The Teacher's Yoke: Studies in Memory of Henry Trantham* (Waco TX: Baylor University Press,1965): 298–304.

_____. "Other Baptist Bodies," in Davis Woolley, ed., *Baptist Advance* (Nashville: Broadman Press, 1964) 368–84.

_____. "The Pauline Church and Support of Missions," in Morris Ashcraft, ed., *Mission Unlimited: Biblical and Doctrinal Foundations* (Nashville: Stewardship Commission, SBC, 1976) 117–50.

_____. "Perspectives in Our Baptist Heritage," in William H. Brackney, ed., *Discovering Our Baptist Heritage* (Valley Forge PA: American Baptist Historical Society, 1985).

_____. "Presbyterian Church," in Cox, vol. 2 of *Encyclopedia of Southern Baptists* (Nashville: Broadman Press, 1958) 1111–12.

_____. "Reformation Sunday," in Charles M. Laymon, ed., *International Lesson Annual* (Nashville: Abingdon Press, 1962) 357–58.

_____. "Religious Scene, New Dimensions of the United States," in Woolley, vol. 3 of *Encyclopedia of Southern Baptists* (Nashville: Broadman Press, 1971) 1940–41.

_____. "Roman Catholic Church," in Cox, vol. 2 of *Encyclopedia of Southern Baptists* (Nashville: Broadman Press, 1958) 1170–72.

_____. *Seminar Sermons* (Liberty, MO: William Jewell College, 1962).

_____. *A Short History of Louisiana Baptists* (Nashville: Broadman Press, 1948).

_____. "Some Reflections on Huguenot History," in *Transactions of the Huguenot Society of South Carolina* 91 (1986).

_____. "Strong, Augustus H.," in Cox, vol. 2 of *Encyclopedia of Southern Baptists* (Nashville: Broadman Press, 1958) 1302–1303.

_____. "The Teaching Church and the Baptist Witness," in *The Truth that Makes Men Free*, report of Eleventh Baptist World Congress (Nashville: Broadman Press, 1965) 341–53.

_____. "Theological Education: Retrospect and Prospect," in *South Carolina Baptist Convention: Book of Messages*, 16–18 November 1977.

II. PERIODICAL ARTICLES

St. Amant, C. Penrose, "Baptist Heritage and Religious Liberty," *The Baptist Training Union Magazine* 39:3 (March 1964): 14–17.

_____. "Baptist Heritage and Religious Liberty," *The Quarterly Review* 23:2 (April 1963): 16–21.

_____. "Baptist History and Citizenship," *The Baptist Training Union Magazine* 39:10 (October 1964): 19–21.

_____. "The Baptist Paper Contending for the Faith," *Arkansas Baptist* (Little Rock AR), 30 March 1961.

_____. "Baptists and Public Education: An Historical Perspective," *The Quarterly Review* 44:1 (January 1984): 66–78.

_____. "Baptists in a Revolutionary Age," *Baptist History and Heritage* 7:3 (July 1972): 137–53.

_____. "Bible Truth for Today's World: Stewardship," *The Sunday School Builder* 45:11 (November 1964): 8.

_____. "Can Christianity Fill Today's Vacuum?" *The Baptist Program*, n.v.n. (March 1962): 21, 23, 27.

_____. "Christ in American History," *The Teacher* 64:7 (July 1950): 2.

_____. "The Christian Ministry and Social Responsibility (with Special Reference to Southern Baptists)," *The Outlook* 21:7 (July 1972): 3–15.

_____. "Christianity and History," four-part series, *The Baptist Student* 32:6 (March 1953): 13–15; 32:7 (April 1953): 26–27; 32:8 (May 1953): 5–6; 32:9 (June 1953): 30–31.

_____. "The Church: A Divine Enterprise," *The Baptist Message* (Alexandria LA), 5 July 1972.

_____. "Comments on Religious Liberty," *The Baptist Message* (Alexandria LA), 14 July 1962.

_____. "Communicating the Gospel in the Eighties," *The Quarterly Review* 41:2 (April 1981): 61–72.

_____. "A Continuing Pilgrimage: A Biographical Sketch of Frank Stagg," *The Theological Educator* 8:1 (Autumn 1977): 37–50.

_____. "Directors on Campus," *The Commission* 36:1 (January 1973): 2.

_____. "Despair Prevails in Luther Country," *The Tie* 34:2 (February 1965): 4.

_____. "The Fallen Torch," *The Baptist Student* 31:8 (May 1952): 25–27.

_____. "God Gets His Man; A Study of Graham Greene," *Perspectives in Religious Studies* 1:1 (Spring 1974): 52–58.

_____. "God, Man, and Redemption in the Writings of Albert Camus," *Review and Expositor* 61:3 (Summer 1964): 156–66.

_____. "Historical Perspective and Biblical Interpretation," *Adult Bible Teaching Guide* 1:1 (October-December 1966): 9–11.

_____. "The Impact of Religion on the Shaping of American Values," *Review and Expositor* 73:1 (Winter 1976): 59–73.

_____. "Is History Made by Heroes?" *Baptist History and Heritage* 1:1 (August 1965): 1–4, 54–55.

_____. "Jimmy Carter's Religious Background," *Neue Zürcher Zeitung* 48:165 (17–19 July 1976).

_____. "Kingdom Citizenship in Action," *Baptist Adults* 3:1 (October 1973): 17–21.

_____. "New Directions in Baptist Colleges and Universities," *Review and Expositor* 64:1 (Winter 1967): 41–47.

_____. "The Next Step in Theological Education," *Arkansas Baptist* (Little Rock), 14 February 1957.

_____. "Of What Use Is History?" *Survey Bulletin for 1964–1965*, Baptist Theological Seminary, Rüschlikon, Switzerland (5 May 1965).

_____. "Our Baptist Heritage," *The Quarterly Review* 10:3 (July 1950): 18–20.

_____. "Our Baptist Heritage and the Church," *Baptist History and Heritage* 2:2 (July 1967): 83–90, 113.

_____. "Our Task," *Baptist History and Heritage* 1:2 (July 1966): 3–6.

_____. "A Pocket Full of Seed," address at Georgetown College, 8 May 1987, *Georgetown Insights* 16:2 (Summer 1987).

_____. "President's Comments," *Rüschlikon Link* (1972–1977).

_____. "The Private World of Theological Students," *Religion in Life* 31:4 (Autumn 1962).

_____. "Reformation: Old and New," *Review and Expositor* 64:2 (Spring 1967): 129–39.

_____. "The Role of the Christian Professor on a University Campus," *The Baptist Faculty Paper* 13:1 (Fall 1969).

_____. "Secular Humanism and the State," *Report from the Capital* 36:5 (May 1981): 9–10.

_____. "The Sheer Joy of Reading," *Student* 59:3 (March 1980): 20–22.

_____. "A Short History of Church History at Southern Baptist Theological Seminary," *Review and Expositor* 82:1 (Winter 1985): 49–63.

_____. "Some Resources for Reconciliation in Our Baptist Heritage," *Baptist Heritage Update* 2:1 (Spring 1986): 5–6.

_____. "Southern Baptist Theology Today: An Interview," *The Theological Educator* 12:2 (Spring 1982): 16–31.

_____. "Southern Baptists and Southern Culture," *Review and Expositor* 67:2 (Spring 1970): 141–52.

_____. "Southern Baptists: Unity in Diversity," *Search* 1:3 (Spring 1971): 6–14.

_____. "A Teacher's Vision," *The Commission* 40:4 (April 1977): 6–10.

_____. "That Night in History," *The Baptist Student* 36:3 (December 1956): 2–4.

_____. "Theological Education and the Denominational Seminary," *Review and Expositor, Special Inaugural Supplement* (Middletown, KY: Western Recorder Press, 1960).

_____. "Toward an Understanding of Culture," *Review and Expositor* 61:1 (Winter 1964): 500–505.

_____. "Undergraduate Education in Historical Perspective," *The Southern Baptist Educator* 48:6 (July 1984): 3–15, 19.

_____. "What Makes A Minister?" *The Baptist Program*, n.v. (August 1970): 25–26.

_____. "What Makes Christianity Unique?" *The Window* 34:12 (August 1963): 4–5, 20.

_____. "Why Are We Here?" *The Baptist Program*, n.v. (January 1968): 4.

_____. "Why Study Church History?" *Vision* 11:3 (November 1954).

III. UNPUBLISHED MANUSCRIPTS, ADDRESSES, AND TAPE RECORDINGS

St. Amant, C. Penrose, "Christian Education in Today's World," Address to Mississippi Baptist Convention, 12 November 1958.

_____. "Christian Education Is Essential," address to Mississippi Baptist Convention, 13 November 1963.

_____. "The Christian Ministry in the 1970s," inaugural address at Baptist Theological Seminary, Rüschlikon, Switzerland, 1972. Unpublished manuscript.

_____. "A Continuing Pilgrimage," sermon on 135th anniversary of First Baptist Church, Shreveport LA, 10 February 1980.

_____. "A Continuing Pilgrimage," sermon on 125th anniversary of First Baptist Church, Monroe LA, 23 September 1979. Unpublished manuscript.

_____. "Education That Lasts," address delivered at inauguration of Joseph C. Clapp as President of the University of Corpus Christi, 1 April 1966. Unpublished manuscript.

_____. "God and the Human Situation," address at Oklahoma Baptist University, 25 September 1968. Unpublished manuscript.

_____. "The Greek Concept of Immortality" (M.A. dissertation, Louisiana State University, 1937).

_____. "A Historical View of Baptist Involvement in Citizenship," paper presented at Christian Citizenship Seminar, Christian Life Commission, SBC, 23 March 1964. Unpublished manuscript.

_____. "If I were a Seminary Graduate Again," commencement address, Golden Gate Baptist Theological Seminary, 14 December 1983. Unpublished manuscript.

_____. "If I were A Seminary Student Again," chapel address, Southern Baptist Theological Seminary, 2 September 1981. Tape recording.

_____. "A Joyful Venture," chapel address, Southern Baptist Theological Seminary, 17 June 1986. Tape recording.

_____. "Liberal Arts Education in a Christian Context," Jones Memorial Lectures, Union University, Jackson TN, 31 October–4 November 1977. Unpublished manuscript.

_____. "Making the Best of a Bad Situation," address to Southern Baptist Theological Seminary, 7 July 1987. Tape recording.

_____. "Martin Luther: The Measure of a Man," address at Golden Gate Baptist Seminary, 2 November 1983. Unpublished manuscript.

_____. "An Outline of the History of Religion in the United States," (n.d.). Unpublished manuscript.

_____. "The Problem of Truth and Error," 1937. Unpublished manuscript.

_____. "Prophetic Preaching in a Secular World," paper presented at New Orleans Ministerial Union, March 1949. Unpublished manuscript.

_____. "The Rise and Early Development of the Princeton School of Theology" (Ph.D. dissertation, Edinburgh University, 1952).

_____. "The Sense of Girls in Sex: A Christian Interpretation," Union Theological Seminary, New York NY, 1944. Unpublished manuscript.

_____. "Some Gnostic Influences on Early Christian Thought" (Th.D. dissertation, New Orleans Baptist Theological Seminary, 1942).

_____. "Strength from Weakness," a sermon preached at Northminster Baptist Church, Jackson MS, 7 July 1984. Unpublished manuscript.

_____. "Together We Serve," address at Southern Baptist Seminary Faculty Retreat, September 1971. Unpublished manuscript.

_____. "The Training of Seminary Students in International Relations," a paper presented at conference of Baptist Joint Committee on Public Affairs, 9–11 October 1968.

_____. "Tribute to Baker James and Eloise Cauthen," presented at Golden Gate Baptist Theological Seminary, 26 March 1981. Tape recording.

ISBN: 0-86554-370-4   H307
AUTHOR: Walter B. Shurden
TITLE: Perspectives on Theological Education
PUBLICATION DATE: 12/11/89   PRICE: $ 13.95
☐ Review copy   ☐ Examination Copy   ☒ Other
                                          Complimentary

This book is sent to you with the compliments of

MERCER UNIVERSITY

 Mercer University Press
MACON • GEORGIA • 31207

We should like to receive two copies of the review and, if possible, a copy of the issue in which it appears.